Tasha Tudor's

Heirloom

Crafts

Tasha Tudor's
Heirloom
Crafts

Text by Tovah Martin

Photographs by Richard W. Brown

Houghton Mifflin Company

Boston   New York

1995

Library of Congress Cataloging-in-Publication Data

Martin, Tovah.

Tasha Tudor's heirloom crafts / text by Tovah Martin ; photographs by Richard W. Brown

p. cm.

ISBN 0-395-73527-0

1. Tudor, Tasha — Themes, motives. 2. Handicraft — United States.

I. Title.

NK839.T84M37 1995   95-18605

745.5'092 — dc20   CIP

SFE 10 9 8 7 6 5 4 3 2 1

Printed in Italy

Book design by Susan McClellan

Color separations by Sfera

ACKNOWLEDGMENTS

Seth Tudor, the woodworker

Guy Wolff, the potter

Rosemary Gladstar, the herbalist

Kate Smith, the weaver

Joan DeGusto, the seamstress

Andy Rice, the shepherd

Amelia Stauffer, the candle-maker

Linda Allen, the marionette maker

Isabelle Hadley, the herbalist

Steve Davie, the gardener

Our gratitude to all the models who patiently lent their time.

CONTENTS

MADE BY HAND

Tasha Tudor and I have been friends for years, and it seems that every time I visit or call, Tasha is engaged with one of her crafts. "I'm making a toy owl," she'll report when I ring in midwinter. "It is beguiling, if I do say so myself." If I suggest that perhaps she'd prefer to talk when she isn't quite so busy, she'll say, "Nonsense, I'm always fiddling with some project or other."

Tasha's hands are never idle, and she has an absolute aversion to sitting still. When I visit in late summer, she can be found bending over the aromatic plants in her herb garden, eradicating weeds. Since anyone who pauses to lend a hand is destined to become a heroine in Tasha's eyes, I generally fall in beside her to help banish whatever culprit happens to be threatening the garden. Anyway, the enterprise never

lasts long, because the conversation strays to the roses she planted last year, and we'll leave the weeding basket behind to go and gather a bouquet.

That's just the beginning, really. After the goats are milked and the biscuits are buttered, Tasha will light a fire to fend off the chill and I'll sit close by, listening to stories about her eccentric relatives while she knits socks. And if socks aren't on the agenda, she'll be knitting lace for the hem of her stiff red petticoats or hand-sewing a dress she designed herself. I watch entranced as she deftly wields her knitting needles, darning needle, or whatever tool happens to be in service at the moment. Often I'll wander in from a stroll to find her perched before her easel, adding the final touches to a watercolor. "Don't be silly," she'll say with a quick wave of the hand. "You're not

bothering me in the least. I'm not an artiste, you know. I don't need to hide away in a studio when I paint. Sit down by the fire." Obediently I draw up a chair beside the hearth, and time slips by as stories are told, retold, and elaborated upon.

I N THE BACK OF MY MIND, I SUPPOSE I always knew that Tasha had a penchant for crafts. After all, when I caught my first glimpse of her, she was jumping down from the front seat of a truck heavily laden with beekeeping equipment. There she was, with full skirts dancing in the breeze and graying braids tied neatly in a kerchief, shuffling around the beehives to keep them from shifting. She had

come to our greenhouse to collect dwarf fuchsias, but we soon learned that another errand was on the docket, because when Tasha returned a few hours later, the truck bed, where the jumble of bee equipment had resided, was piled with handwoven baskets. Apparently she had bartered beeware for baskets, and her time-weathered cheeks were flushed with victory.

Tasha has a penchant for melon baskets because they're easy to tote, but she confesses that this miniature "won't carry much more than a few tightly packed berries." She did the intricate weaving herself, using black ash harvested on the property.

She unloaded a few baskets, explained the finer points of each, and drove off. I like to think that even if I hadn't known of Tasha Tudor's reputation and her fame as a children's illustrator, I would have realized then and there that I had just met a very singular character indeed.

Being a gardener in heart and soul, I was preoccupied during my initial visits to Corgi Cottage with the outdoors. I would spend every precious moment ambling along the vine-embowered paths that thread through the terraces, picking my way past vines that groped overhead, following the wildflower walk down to the water-lily pond when the noonday sun beat too radiantly. To be sure, I concentrated the bulk of my attention on the cinnamon pinks in blossom. But I couldn't help but notice that the interior of Tasha's hand-hewn house brimmed with the most exquisite paraphernalia I had ever encountered.

There is a great deal to appreciate when you visit Tasha Tudor, and I'm not the only one to say so. When you first come indoors from the garden, it takes quite a few minutes for your eyes to adjust to the ambient darkness. Even on the sunniest days, the house is a warm but subdued place. And Tasha is forever moving about, especially when tea is being served, telling riveting tales that demand your full attention as she performs her many tasks. So there is scarcely a spare minute to take stock of the surroundings until a thunderstorm comes up and Tasha is preoccupied elsewhere. Then, when you make your way through the maze of tiny

Incredible aromas waft forth when Tasha begins working in the kitchen, and all sorts of intriguing antique cooking paraphernalia — some inherited, some acquired — also appear, including tin cookie cutters of various shapes and carved wooden butter molds.

rooms, you begin to fathom the full breadth and scope of Tasha's affection for collectibles, as well as what incredible objects her own hands have wrought.

Every nook and cranny of Tasha's house holds something admirable hidden in its shadows. There are more wooden kegs than you can imagine and more baskets than anyone could possibly employ in a single lifetime. Old crocks filled with grains or animal treats are set in every corner; handwoven linens are spread on any surface that might gather dust; antique tools of every description and purpose are hung where they might be found in haste; and immense looms — seven, at last count — take up any spare

floor space. But the most amazing aspect of it all is that Tasha is busy making all the many crafts that you find scattered about.

I've often wondered at Tasha's incredible industriousness. She's not a nervous person, by

---

Tasha never tires of sewing dresses for her doll, Emma, and redesigning the dollhouse decor. But "you can't change clothes on a marionette," she explains. "You have to make a whole new puppet for each scene."

anyone's definition of the term. She simply prefers to keep her hands occupied. "Just as you like to garden, I enjoy making things," she explains. But I have a theory. I've always suspected that this busyness stems from her Yankee upbringing. Many Yankees that I've encountered insist on occupying every minute of their lives productively, utilizing all the resources at their disposal. And Tasha has honed this propensity to a science. If a varmint runs off with a guinea hen in the night, she gathers the telltale feathers and sews them into toys.

Everything in Tasha's life has a purpose. The lushness of her flowerbeds is orchestrated primarily for the benefit of her artwork. "That rose has figured in more posters than I care to count," she assures anyone whose hair becomes snagged in a particularly rambunctious rambler. Everything earns its keep. Even the corgyn (that's the plural of corgi, according to Tasha) that romp around your heels are good for something, I'm certain. The one-eyed cat also probably serves some productive function, although she catches precious few chipmunks, I've noticed. The goats, the gardens, the wooden snow shovel, the chickens that strut about — everything originally had a purpose. And everything is interwoven. The garden furnishes dried herbs to keep the goats healthy  during the winter, the goats supply milk for the cheese served to guests, and the forest supplies kindling for the stove, which bakes pies to feed Tasha, who milks the goats, makes the cheese, stokes the fire, and weeds the herb garden (with help from guests). All the parts of Tasha's life work comfortably together.

While dinner is simmering on the stove, Tasha slips into the next room and weaves a little of the fifteen-yard piece of linen that will someday line her quilted petticoats. "I might finish the job in a few weeks if I could devote some consecutive hours to the project," she says, sighing.

As far as Tasha is concerned, crafts are for sharing, and her home is a frequent meeting place for craftspeople of great fame. Friends are at her elbow when it's time to thread the loom or bake bread in the beehive oven, they help stoke the fires for the kettle of wax when candles are dipped, and they keep the corgyn at bay when the lard is being heated for soap.

So every once in a while craftspeople gather at Tasha's to share, learn, and keep their crafts alive. It's a beautiful thing to behold, but it has a bittersweet edge. Many of the activities that take place at Corgi Cottage are sorely in danger of slipping into the forgotten arts. Sad though it may seem, most people cannot see why anyone would want to spend a day standing over a smoking cauldron dipping candles; they wonder what might provoke someone to waste energy pounding an ash sapling merely to acquire a handful of basket-weaving strips. Not many people scutch and hackle flax anymore,

Tucked here and there at Corgi Cottage are all sorts of handmade things that might fascinate a child. "That's just an old pull toy," Tasha says of the rolling puppy beside the hearth. But children's eyes invariably light up when they see the results of past craftsmanship.

or know what those words mean.

I have noticed that Tasha always invites several grandchildren and their young friends when she's making cider, weaving fences, or doing something else that can benefit from their muscle. They ramble through the tiny rooms in the farmhouse, looking at all the splendid toys and imagining how each tool might be used. They admire the dollhouse and the marionettes and eat scrumptious pies. But most important, they spend several long hours watching the choreography and intricate movements of hands that are never idle. And they witness the incredible crafts that result.

CHAPTER ONE

CRAFTS FROM THE LAND

BASKETRY ❧ WOODWORKING ❧ POTTERY

WHEN YOU FIRST TURN IN to Tasha's long and scenic driveway, you see the rather handsome forest that skirts the road's twistings and turnings. And when you come close to the cottage, before you are immersed in the lupine meadow or catch a glimpse of the big barn, you become aware of the fragrance of the wood smoke that spirals gracefully from the chimney. The scent from the wood-burning stove follows you wherever you go.

Several years ago, someone took an axe to an exquisitely gnarled apple tree at the far end of Tasha's meadow, and she is still distressed. "The youth who performed the dirty deed was directed merely to trim a few extraneous limbs, and he took it into his head to remove the en-

tire tree," she explains. "I was truly dismayed." From that moment, Tasha has been wary of permitting anyone but trusted friends and relatives to bring cutting devices of any description onto her property.

Tasha was not the only resident of her mountaintop to mourn the loss of the apple tree; a family of bluebirds was also deeply affected. "It was their favorite nesting spot," she often says wistfully, "and when it was removed, they never came back here again." With an uncommon affection for anything feathered, Tasha sees trees not only as canopies of shade during the summer and retainers of soil during mud season but also as shelters and perches for her winged companions. If a tree has a hollow limb, all the better for a resident titmouse or flicker.

Tasha's hilltop is generously wooded with a thick stand of white pine, fir, beech, swamp maple, ash, and birch. When she visited Emerson's home in Concord, Massachusetts, she pocketed a chestnut; it successfully sprouted, and the resulting tree spreads its limbs in the field not far from the clothesline. Just footsteps from the chicken yard stands a fledgling English oak that has grown from an acorn her son Tom picked up in Sherwood Forest. But

most of the property looks like the surrounding countryside.

Even though plenty of timber is available for heating and baking, Tasha obtains her fuel from a neighbor rather than from her own splendid forest. And she definitely likes to keep her home toasty. "There's no point in being chilly," she declares while feeding the fire with kindling. When I phone, there's invariably an interruption at some point or other in the conversation while she attends to the stove. "Now you just hold the line one minute while I check the fires," she says, and I hear the brisk patter of her step as she hustles into another room, followed by the scraping of the cast-iron stove door.

Tasha tends the fires personally. The body of the house is warmed by a hardworking cook-

Vermont forests provide cordwood for warmth in winter as well as the raw material for many crafts. Even some of the tools Tasha uses, like this shaving horse, are hand-hewn from native lumber.

Growing up in old farmhouses, Seth had ample opportunity to study traditional construction techniques. No one would guess that the post-and-beam barn he raised singlehandedly was not several hundred years old.

stove supplemented by two open fireplaces, which are pressed into service on chilly mornings and bitter evenings. The whole enterprise requires a generous stash of fuel.

Firing the cookstove is quite a delicate science. After all, the heat must remain constant if the baked goods are to be perfect. Tasha's standard response to anyone who doubts the pru-dence of cooking with wood fuel is "I can bake an angel food cake quite successfully — hard and dry wood is what is needed for the task." The proof, of course, is demonstrated when dessert is served and everyone begs for seconds.

The fires are a chore, to be sure, but Tasha's house was definitely constructed to endure the elements. Anyone who has ever managed to reach the top of the mountain in midwinter will attest to the fact that the house is quite snug. Just in case a stray draft should happen by, every chair in every room is conveniently draped with a hand-knit shawl to throw over your shoulders if need be. But to be honest, I've never detected the slightest breeze penetrating the interior of Tasha's farmhouse. In fact, the

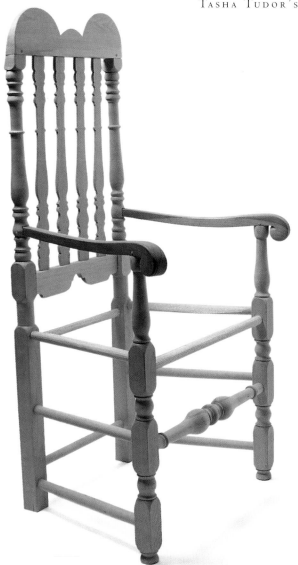

ago by Tasha's son Seth. The aura of age was wholly intentional — both mother and son set out to create an environment that seemed retrospective in every sense. For the design, Tasha chose a 1740 farmhouse that she admired in Concord, New Hampshire. Seth made several trips to the farmhouse, took measurements, and proceeded to reproduce its plan faithfully. However, one major alteration was necessary. The floor plan had to be reversed so the house could perch proudly on the summit of Tasha's mountain without any redistribution of the land, because, as Tasha so poetically points out, "Seth was uncomfortable with the employment of explosives."

Not only was the result a faithful recreation of the original, but the building process was carried out in an authentically eighteenth-century manner. All of the many boards for the rambling cottage are native hemlock and pine that was sawed at a mill close by. That was the only time that electric power came into play on the project. There was no electricity in Tasha's remote neck of the woods when the house was being constructed or for several years thereafter, so Seth did the work entirely with hand tools, spending endless evenings sitting around with his brother, Tom, and patiently whittling oak pins to hold the beams in position. He did all the masonry, and Tom all the shingling. "It was an adventure," Seth recalls, "like reading a good book. You always have a notion what the end will be, but there's suspense in following the plot." The finished product is a marvel of skill

cottage retains a coziness that draws you back into its heart when you haven't visited for a month or two. Every hand-cut floorboard, every joist and beam of the mortise-and-tenon structure, exudes the sort of hominess usually found only in houses that have been in existence for several hundred years.

Tasha's home certainly seems very old in both body and spirit. It has the soul of a place that has nurtured many generations safely within its walls. But in truth, it was built merely twenty-two years

When Seth works on a reproduction, he studies every curve of the original. Then he goes out, cuts down a tree, and turns the wood on his lathe, just as furniture-makers did centuries ago.

and engineering, especially when you consider that Seth never had any formal training in his trade. But really, if he has an uncanny skill for carpentry, it's little wonder. One of his grandfathers, William Starling Burgess, was a naval architect who designed racing yachts that defended the World Cup.

WHEN TACKLING THE INEVITABLE problems posed by building a house with few assistants and no power tools, Seth used his inherent talent to approach the task creatively and cost-effectively. (Like his mother, he is every inch a Yankee.) When it came time to raise the huge timbers of the barn, he rummaged through the dump to find parts he could use to make an ingenious crane capable of shouldering the burden. Seth and his crane did what usually calls for the help of several dozen strong neighbors and brought the heavy wooden frame to its feet. "It looked just magnificent, like a skeleton ship," Tasha recalls.

All told, it took Seth three years to build the cottage. When the exterior was completed, he set to work indoors, performing the finishing work, laying intentionally crooked sills and hanging doors just slightly askew. For him, the house's character lies in its charming faults. "There is no work of art that hath not some imperfection in its lines," he quotes, while ducking to avoid hitting his forehead on a deliberately low-slung door frame. Of course, Tasha helped with the construction, her main responsibility being to lay the floorboards, "which is why they have such cavernous gullies between the planks. We used native lumber, and it shrank. I always threaten to drop poppy seeds in the cracks and have a garden." Tasha was also responsible for some of the window frames, which have withstood the stresses of time more successfully. However, when the weather turns foul, every frame is carefully fitted with a snug storm window secured by wooden pegs. The result is a home that looks ages old, both indoors and out. "It could fool

most people, don't you think?" Tasha often asks me. "Unless they've read one of your books, of course."

INSIDE, THE HOUSE IS A MAZE OF SMALL rooms, tight corridors, and many doors leading into further hidden rooms. I have been to Tasha's home many, many times over the years, and yet I am continually discovering still another place that I haven't dreamed existed. The house is filled with the furniture Tasha has been collecting since she attended her first auction at sixteen and brought home quite a bargain. "No one wanted to outbid such a sweet young thing," she explains with a mischievous grin.

Seth shares his mother's admiration for good furniture. If you walk through the woods to his cottage, you'll find the carpenter in his.workshop, creating reproductions that have all the eccentricities and character of the early American originals. The turnings will be a tad lopsided, just like the originals, and the beveling and silhouettes are also lovingly copied. The beauty lies not only in the furniture's graceful lines but in the fact that it was built to last.

Everything in Tasha's house performs its function and addresses its purpose admirably. The chairs lean forward to keep their occupants writing or sewing or concentrating on the task at hand. Cabinets with mesh doors and rough shelves were constructed specifically to hold jars of preserved fruit.

Although Tasha did her part to finish the house and knows the use and potential of many obscure objects offered at neighborhood yard sales, she is not a carpenter by any definition of the term. "I've built an occasional flat box when the need has arisen. But Seth will arrive and show me a much easier route than the method I've devised to join the wood." She also

In winter, grain to feed the animals is transported into the barn on an old wooden sled. Safely indoors, it is stored in wooden barrels. Tasha's favorite is made from a massive hollow log.

---

hammered together a rather fancy chicken coop to protect her precious birdies. But for the most part, she prefers appreciation to construction where wood is concerned.

And her appreciation is not casual. You have to assume that everything Tasha owns serves some valuable function. The trick lies in guessing what everything does — and why it's there. There are various and sundry chests, barrels, kegs, scoops, and buckets for every conceivable purpose, as well as all sorts of utensils employed at some time or other to accomplish farming tasks. There's a curious boomerang-shaped gadget for stretching deerskins; many shovels, including a wooden snow shovel that when properly waxed performs its duty better than the cheap aluminum versions; several hayforks; rakes of all descriptions; and a flail for threshing grain — "a wickedly fanged instrument indeed," Tasha readily affirms. She also has a prodigious collection of yokes designed to fit petite shoulders and ease the chore of fetching water. After all, Tasha had no indoor plumbing for six years, "and it always seemed that the animals were thirstier in sub-zero weather."

Tasha isn't terribly fond of trinkets or anything that lacks a good useful purpose. If she didn't use baskets daily to fetch vegetables to the kitchen or to carry the laundry to the line, she wouldn't waste a moment weaving them, you can be sure. But the fact is that she is always calling baskets into service, and so she has a healthy respect for them.

BEFORE WE PROCEED ANY FURTHER, it should be said that Tasha never refers to basket-making or quilting or weaving or any of the other tasks that she undertakes as "crafts." In fact, she dislikes the word intensely and made quite a fuss when she first

When Tasha tackles a basket, she generally means it to carry a sizable load. "Even when the ash is well soaked, coaxing it through the splints is no easy feat."

caught wind of this book's title. "I don't do crafts," she said firmly. "Well then, how shall we describe the things you do?" I asked with trepidation. "Call them anything you like, but not crafts," she responded, with determination in her voice. We racked our brains to think of a proper term to describe the handiwork in question, but we couldn't find another word to suit. So Tasha finally agreed that "crafts" would have to do.

All her life, Tasha has admired baskets. But it wasn't until twenty years ago that she decided

biscuits, crackers, peanut butter, and other delectables fill her cupboards or are set close at hand (if they contain snacks of any sort). They come in all shapes and sizes, with handles and without, with lids and open. Her favorite is a quart-size butter churn that sits in constant readiness on her kitchen counter.

Guy tells me that in the old days, the colonies weren't permitted to turn out stoneware, which was considered a fine craft, so American crocks were originally imported from Britain. After the Revolutionary War, potteries sprang up everywhere, but they all initially used a pale gray clay that came from South Amboy, New Jersey. "So the lighter gray stoneware comes from city potteries, and the

darker pieces were thrown at rural shops, where local clays were mixed in," Guy explains as he fixes yet another lump of clay on his wheel and starts it swiftly rotating.

BESIDES HER FLOWERPOTS AND STONE-ware crocks, Tasha owns several sets of china, some of which makes an appearance every afternoon when tea is served. No matter how busy Tasha happens to be, no matter where she has just come from or where she is scheduled to go, there is always time for tea.

No one has to be coaxed when the aroma of freshly baked scones begins floating through the house. Everyone takes a tray and helps carry the scones, cookies, and cakes down the wind-

Both Tasha's and Guy's forebears sailed clipper ships to China. "These porcelains were all painted by children," Guy explains. "The early designs were simple and precise, but with time and popularity they became very abstract."

ing paths to the wisteria- and clematis-covered bower on the lower terrace. In midsummer, a rustic wooden table and chairs await, fuchsias blossom all around, and several terra-cotta pots surround the alcove. If everyone lends a hand, the table is soon covered with food, silverware, gracefully folded cloth napkins, and china. Tea usually lasts quite a while. It is a leisurely affair, and Tasha will not have it otherwise.

After the meal is over, things are cleared away and the empty china is carried back to the kitchen. "May I help with the dishes?" I ask. "All right," Captain Pegler, the parrot, answers from the birdcage near the sink, in a tone uncannily like Tasha's. So I slip the cups carefully beneath Tasha's copper faucet, soap, rinse, and dry them, and hang them on their hooks in the cupboard to wait to grace another meal.

CHAPTER TWO

FIELD AND GARDEN

HERBS ❧ DRIED FLOWERS ❧ FLAX

ALL OF TASHA'S CRAFTS TIE IN TO her art. The dresses she stitches, the baskets she weaves, and even the marionettes she makes show up somewhere in her illustrations. Tasha has always drawn from her life. The goats, her grandchildren, the cocky rooster and his hens, even the butter churn and the spinning wheel appear in the pages of her books. There's plenty to portray, because Tasha spends endless hours crafting beautiful things so she never needs to fabricate from her imagination. All those fantastic floral borders and blossom-packed wreaths that run around the margins of her books are painted from real-life examples. "You should see the wreath I've made as a model for the bookplate," she'll say with pride. "It's a dandy, full of apples, rosebuds, and berries."

Tasha makes bouquets in all sizes from modest to magnificent. On the modest side, every birdcage in her home contains at least one miniature bouquet, carefully arranged and replenished every day after the birds have torn it to bits. More ambitious floral extravaganzas that might compete favorably with the efforts of any professional florist are set proudly in the parlor when important company is expected. In spring Tasha composes little tussie-mussies for lucky friends by bunching together violets and other fragrant flowers, placing them in a collar of aromatic herbs, and tying them with ribbons. Later in the season she strings lovely garlands of daisies in overlapping chains for the children to wear as crowns at her midsummer party.

Finding flowers to act as models is simple

in summer, when all the hours spent weeding and pouring manure tea on the terraces bear fruit. Although Tasha never plants with a certain illustration in mind, she always keeps a vigilant eye out for promising portrait-worthy blossoms. During the growing season, more flowers qualify than she can possibly find time to paint. However, in winter, securing models is not quite so simple.

E
VEN IN JANUARY, TASHA'S GREEN-house is studded with blooms. With sufficient sun, the geraniums hold forth throughout the year, and there is a steady supply of camellias from bushes selected to extend the display for as many months as possible. But Tasha often requires more blossoms to model for a particularly lush painted border. For that purpose, she sometimes turns to dried flowers.

Other than the occasional sentimental four-leaf clover, pansy, or rosebud pressed between the pages of *The Oxford Book of English Verse*, dried flowers are not among Tasha's favorites. If asked the reason for her feelings, she quotes

Every floral border that ever ran around one of Tasha's greeting cards was once a living wreath. In earliest spring, primroses and flowering bulbs are enlisted as models. In winter, Tasha resorts to dried larkspur, strawflowers, zinnias, peonies, and herbs.

from Shakespeare: "At Christmas I no more desire a rose than wish a snow in May's newfangled mirth." She prefers to admire each flower in its season. She would much rather use the living, growing parts of plants to render into pictures and fill vases around the house, and she summons all her resources toward that goal. The Advent wreath on the front door is a medley of evergreens, and her Christmas wreath is made from boxwood sprigs woven together to form a dense circle of glossy greenery. Because Tasha is a Yankee and fond of nature's rhythms, she shrinks from artificiality.

As a rule, she doesn't grow flowers for drying. One year she planted the vegetable garden with strawflowers, larkspur, lamb's ears,

and statice especially for that purpose. It was quite a sight to behold, because Tasha always goes all out. She harvested bushels of flowers when their buds were just unfolding, to retain the best color, and picked them early in the morning, when the stems were at their fullest, to insure straight posture after they were dried. Then she bundled them into fistfuls, tied the bunches with raffia, and hung them upside down in the warm kitchen, where they were her pride and joy for a while. But eventually she grew weary of seeing these everlastings perennially dangling overhead. When it comes to horticulture, Tasha prefers a constantly changing scene. By the time Christmas came around, most of the dried flowers had gone into arrangements and been sent off to friends. However, a few vestiges were suffered to stay, and they remain, hanging from the beams and adding a spark of color to the pantry no matter how gloomy it is outside.

THE DRIED FLOWERS ARE NOT THE only plants to dangle from the beams. If you happen to be tall, you're bound to bump into several dozen bunches of different herbs suspended in the pantry too, within easy reach when Tasha is making broth for soup. Toward spring, you'll do considerably less ducking, because the bundles slowly dwindle as they are called on to season various dishes. By summer, there are noticeable gaps and the stock is sorely in need of replenishing. Then Tasha goes out with a pair of kitchen shears in one hand and her beloved harvest basket in the other to gather more herbs.

The herb garden commands the crest of a hill and is surrounded by a mass of poppies. The hillside site, with its lean soil and excellent drainage, is ideal for the herbs that Tasha uses daily. In fact, the essential oils of most herbs are strongest when the plants aren't overfed. Planted in a formal style, with a brick walk skirting the circular bed and a potted bay or rosemary standard in the center, Tasha's herb garden is the most neatly groomed nook on the premises. And no wonder — its owner is out there daily with her scissors, clipping away at the winter savory, tarragon, marjoram, dill, sweet basil, garlic chives, or whatever she needs to enliven one of her recipes. She uses most of the harvest fresh, but the surplus is preserved for the future.

Thyme is Tasha's most frequent target when she goes out with a basket in hand. "I never have enough thyme," she mutters, glancing at me to make sure I have caught her pun. "I cut it unmercifully for drying," she confesses. But sooner or later all the herbs are cut to come indoors, and the remaining stems just branch out and become bushier, adding to the prevailing profusion.

Born with a liking for anything practical, Tasha makes good use of every herb she can

---

Although the greenhouse is a confection of flowers throughout the cold months, it has its practical aspects and nurtures the herbs that Tasha uses daily. In summer, strawberry pots spilling with herbs sit not far from the kitchen on the upper terrace.

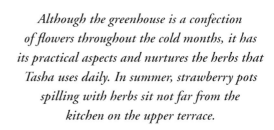

lay her hands on. She adds sage to hard cheese and turkey stuffing. Basil goes into the baked bean recipe of which she is inordinately proud. Vast quantities of parsley are cut, chopped, and frozen for future use. Bay leaves, which she adds to soups and stews, sit in a large bowl on the dresser. But most herbs are sheared, bunched into small handfuls, tied, and hung to dry. Eventually they end up overhead in the kitchen, but they are dried in the rafters of the attic or greenhouse.

Root herbs, such as burdock and carrots, are a different story, of course. They are prepared in a vegetable dryer. Tasha does have a newfangled version, but it is rarely called into service. More often you'll find the large rectangular antique dryer sitting on the woodstove, laboring away. It takes the better part of the day to work its magic, "but it does a superb job."

Some of the herbs Tasha harvests go into her recipes, and others are for tea. Tasha herself does not take herb tea with meals. Instead, she serves a "good black tea" with a considerable kick; Irish Breakfast is her favorite. But she does take herb tea occasionally for her constitution.

Dried herbs also come into play when Tasha makes one of her salves or creams. As far as I can tell, she rarely purchases cosmetics. Once in a while she might indulge in an exceptionally good bottle of English violet cologne. By and large, she prefers to use creams and ointments that she has made herself. A little stash

If a guest asks for herb tea, Tasha fetches a mixture of chamomile, spearmint, rose petals, rosehips, and blue malva, which is every bit as beautiful and aromatic as any potpourri.

of glass jars and apothecary bottles filled with that sort of thing conveniently waits in the bathroom when you visit.

T ASHA'S BATHROOM IS A FINE AFFAIR by anyone's standards. An astonishingly ornate Staffordshire bowl with a very substantial-looking chain pull sits in one corner with a note attached to warn the uninitiated about the evils of yanking too hard on the chain. Close by stands a cage filled with twittering zebra and nun finches. A prodigious copper tub large enough to bathe an entire family ("Its former owner employed it as a water trough for the cows") takes up a generous portion of one wall. There's a dresser, where

February sunlight illuminates bottles filled with herbal remedies and scents. For soothing winter's chapped hands, Tasha uses a homemade lotion of aloe, lanolin, and calendula from the garden.

Tasha's combs and hairpins are neatly laid out in readiness; a chair, where her robes and nightgowns are hung when not in use; and a French porcelain sink in a polished black walnut cabinet, with all manner of soaps, creams, oils, and toilet waters sitting before the mirror.

Anyone who has ever met Tasha will agree that she is not a vain person. Certainly she is invariably neatly clad, with carefully color-

seed, and that's not far from the truth. One year she decided to plant flax, which she then harvested, spun, dyed, wove, and sewed into a checked shirt for her brother. The process took three years from seed to shirt, and it required quite a bit of obscure equipment and a good deal of research. Not only that, but it has a wonderfully arcane vocabulary all its own. If you happen to overhear Tasha and her weaving friend, Kate Smith, talking about flax, it sounds a bit as if they are speaking a foreign language until you're privy to the terms.

FIRST THE FIELD OF FLAX IS PLANTED thickly, so the stalks grow up straight and tall, wedged between their brethren. "Oh, but it's a lovely sight, with the tall stems bowing and dancing in the breezes and the sky-blue flowers," Tasha recalls. When the crop reaches a yard in height, it is harvested, roots and all. The stalks are bundled, dried, and rippled with a wooden comb to remove the seedpods. Then someone hitches up her skirts, wades into the pond, and submerges the bundles, weighing them down with stones. Even after the flax has soaked for five days, it does

When the flax's soft, silky fibers are finally liberated, they must be combed through a series of hatchels with increasingly fine teeth. When not in use, the hatchel's pronged bed is stored safely in a wooden box.

not willingly surrender its fiber. The silky contents of each stalk must be tortured out of their husk, and that calls for a flax brake, a fascinatingly primitive piece of equipment that works like a massive wooden jaw, pounding the stems until they're broken. Then something called a swingle knife is applied rather brutally to beat the fibers free. Finally, after much violence, the fibers are liberated, but you must comb them clean and straight by flinging them through a nasty-looking bed of tines known as a hatchel.

TASHA INHERITED HER FLAX WHEEL, which sits in the parlor with the distaff dressed with a wad of flax ready to be spun whenever she can find a spare moment. But the braking, swingling, and hackling process can take a full day and requires the assistance of someone with strong shoulders, which is why Kate is called in for the event. Spinning is definitely a more leisurely affair and can be accomplished now and then while waiting for a pot to boil. "It's very relaxing," Tasha often says, "and fulfilling as well."

Spinning, I have discovered, is not as easy as it looks. "There's a whole art to dressing the distaff," Tasha assures me when I ask about the preliminaries. I must take her word for that, because the distaff is always quite well dressed when I come, which leaves only the actual art of spinning to master. You operate the flax wheel by sitting on a chair with one foot on the treadle, one hand pulling the fibers from the distaff and the other pulling the threads away

"It's one thing to spin flax, but getting a good even thread is another matter entirely," Tasha often says. "Slip your shoes off," she suggests, "and you'll soon master the rhythm of the wheel."

from the rotating bobbin as they wind and are fed in. Every once in a while you dip your fingers in a hollow gourd with a little water in its belly to moisten the strands. "Originally, spinsters wet the flax with their saliva, but you may prefer water," Tasha calls from the kitchen as I try my hand at the wheel.

The endeavor requires an incredible amount of dexterity and rhythm. When Tasha handles the wheel, her fiber is methodically spun into a perfectly even thread. Mine is so full of thickenings and sparse sections that she discreetly removes it the moment I finish, lest anyone imagine that she produced such an inferior product. The secret, she repeatedly claims, lies in performing the task slowly. "That's all right," she says, comforting me. "Your talents lie in gardening rather than turning plants into textiles." She is probably right.

CHAPTER THREE

ALL CREATURES
GREAT AND SMALL

DAIRYING   ❧   SOAP- AND CANDLE-MAKING   ❧   WOOL

T HE EVIDENCE OF TASHA'S fondness for animals is all over her property. In fact, Corgi Cottage could be described as a farm, I suppose, although it's much more floriferous than any farm I've ever seen. When you drive up, you are greeted by the bleating of goats and the cackling of chickens as well as the noises of various and sundry other fowl.

The place looks like a farm, sounds like a farm, and functions like a farm, too. Every creature that you encounter on Tasha's little mountaintop is there for a practical reason. Even if the animals in residence don't do something obviously useful, like providing suste-

nance for guests, Tasha has dreamed up some creative way for them to earn their keep.

For example, some folks might not immediately think that chickens have anything to do with crafts. But Tasha can easily prove such skeptics wrong. She is terribly fond of birds, and chickens seem to be among her favorites. I suspect that she would use any excuse to have a few chickens hanging about, and she definitely keeps more hens than she needs to supply eggs for custard and ornaments and feathers to adorn toys.

Every year, whether she needs more birds or not, she sends to a hatchery that specializes in rare breeds and arranges for the chicks to be sent by post. The freshly hatched bantams receive extraordinary care; they are scarcely larger than bumblebees when they arrive and must be protected from the elements and other unfriendly factors. First and foremost, their pen is always covered with a screen, because the corgyn apparently cannot resist temptation. The entire troupe is carted outdoors if the sun is shining and the temperature is high enough, and then gathered in Tasha's apron and hustled back indoors at the first hint of a thunderstorm or a stiff breeze. If the chicks do get wet, Tasha carefully rubs their fluff dry with towels. In the evening and on chilly days, they are warmed by crocks of hot water. Tasha abhors heat lamps, because they can cause a fire if jostled.

E VENTUALLY THE BIRDS GROW UP AND fend for themselves, giving the resident canines a run for their money if need be. Still, they must be locked up every evening before dark in their coop, the rather elaborate affair that Tasha constructed herself, and let loose every morning at cockcrow.

Guinea hens are particularly foolish about refusing Tasha's protective measures, and she has lost many to raccoons, although Winslow feels certain that foxes are the culprits. Whoever the marauders might be, Tasha salvages any vestiges of her precious poultry and puts the remnants to good use. Guinea hen feathers often provide plumage for her toy horned owls and festoon the other toys that she spends her winter hours making.

In addition to the exotic breeds, Tasha keeps a good supply of plain old Rhode Island Reds

(she had twenty-nine at last count) for egg production, which is a serious business for her. "I collected nine eggs in the pullet nest this morning," she reports in autumn with the glow of achievement. Later in the season, her pleasure in the plenitude begins to wear thin, and she becomes quite generous with the output from her cottage industry. "My chickies are such proud layers — can I interest you in a few dozen?" she says, a tinge of urgency in her tone. The Federal Express man is rewarded with several cartons whenever he hazards the drive up, and so is anyone who performs similar heroics during mud season. When the situation becomes truly dire, Tasha buries the excess under her rosebushes, which isn't as wacky as it sounds — the eggs eventually break down and provide phosphorous to fertilize the shrubs above.

Tasha uses her hens' eggs liberally in custards, cakes, mayonnaise, and most of her other recipes, sniffing in disdain at the slightest mention of cholesterol. In spring, she decorates the extras and hangs them on the Easter bush. Of course, her bush in no way resembles the slapdash affairs found on some suburban front lawns. Preparation for this extravaganza begins

The elaborate chicken coop that Tasha built for her layers boasts many ingenious features, such as an entrance that few other creatures can fit through. The feathers of guinea hens that fail to seek its safety end up as part of Tasha's toys.

in February, when Tasha dons snowshoes to retrieve a birch sapling from the forest. The sapling is brought back to the warmth of the greenhouse, where it spends several weeks with its stem plunged in a huge cistern filled with water. Foliage begins to sprout just in time for Easter, or as Tasha puts it, "Lovely little tender green leaves spring willingly forth, with no trouble whatsoever!" In the meantime, Tasha has been delicately puncturing holes in the tops and bottoms of her excess eggs, blowing out their contents, and cutting snippets of colored paper to glue on the surfaces in decoupage. The eggs are finished with taffeta ribbons attached to the top so they can swing gracefully from the limbs of the birch sapling. "It isn't as

easy as it appears," Tasha assures anyone who isn't watching with the proper degree of awe. "Eggshells are very frail, you know. One false move and they're shattered."

Tasha has always preferred brown eggs — "New Englanders like brown eggs, and New Yorkers favor white ones" — so she has to trade with a neighbor if she wants eggs to dye for Easter. After tying sprigs of grass or herbs onto the shells, she uses natural dyes (usually onion skins) to color the eggs; when she removes the sprigs, a silhouetted pattern remains. Other eggs also get into the act. She empties duck eggs ("They have a shell like leather") of their contents, snips an oval from the side, and arranges a scene inside — a little wooden bird, perhaps, nestled on a bed of moss. These are then strung by a ribbon from the Easter bush. Depending on what birds happen to be in residence, the bush is bedecked with peacock, pigeon, canary, bantam, ring-necked dove, and finch eggs, too.

I CAN MANAGE TO HOLD MY OWN IN A conversation about chickens, but when it comes to goats, Tasha and I are more firmly on common ground. We have both kept dairy goats for many, many years, and we often phone to compare notes when a doe hasn't come into heat on schedule in autumn or when there's a complication with kidding in spring. The great gap between us, however, is that I prefer Saanens and Tasha is partial to Nubians.

Sometimes I suspect that Tasha pooh-poohs

Before the goats produce quarts of creamy milk, they must be bred, which takes place in autumn. "I suspect that my Bucky might be a wimp," Tasha worries. "The girls certainly aren't enamored of his charms."

my Saanen herd because the progeny are so predictable. Every year I get pure white kids. Her breeding yields more varied results, but she seems to strive for shades of brown, similar to the coloration and markings of deer. Her goats are adorable, by any definition of the word, with Roman noses and oversized floppy ears. But the fawnlike markings can lead to problems when hunting season rolls around. Not to be outwitted by marksmen who might stray past her NO HUNTING signs, Tasha makes sure her herd wears rather large, rather loud, bright pink ribbons in autumn. The more deerlike goats are given several such bows — one around the neck, another girding the midriff. "Belly bands," Tasha calls them.

Twice a day the goats obediently mount their stanchion and give milk, so much that Tasha has plenty to make ice cream, butter, and cheese. Every pat of homemade butter is imprinted by her presses.

Tasha's goats are large animals compared to most Nubians, and they produce a generous quantity of creamy milk. There are seven goats at present, although only two or three are milking at any given time. Like all of Tasha's animals, they live a charmed existence. Tasha gives them beet greens in season and plenty of alfalfa hay. She dries comfrey and maple leaves for their wintertime delectation. And when

cider is being pressed, she tosses buckets of apple mash over the fence, bellowing a brisk "Treats, ladies . . . move out of the way!"

Every day the goats are milked at seven in the morning and again at seven in the evening. They are herded out into their large wooded pasture in the morning in good weather and returned to their nice snug barn faithfully at dusk. In between, if there is even a hint of drizzle, they are brought indoors immediately, because to a goat, the only fate worse than death is getting damp.

NEEDLESS TO SAY, THERE IS EXTRA milk most of the time, and the surplus goes into cheese. The corgyn are apparently addicted to freshly made cottage cheese generously seasoned with garlic and sage. To make it, Tasha takes a gallon of goats' milk, heats it to 175° F, cools it to 72° F, adds rennet, and lets it sit overnight. The next morning she awakens to find a nice junket. She strains the curds through a cheesecloth, hangs them to drip dry, then adds cream, garlic, and herbs. "Don't the dogs object to garlic?" I inquire. "Oh, they adore it," she insists.

Hard cheese is made with a more complex recipe. "There are all sorts of cheeses," Tasha proclaims when you ask how to make hard cheese. "Cheddar is the most difficult." They all entail collecting two gallons of milk, pouring it into the blue enamel French kettle ("an aluminum pan will not work"), and heating it to 72° F. Then Tasha adds the culture and lets the cheese set. When it is fairly firm, she cuts

When frigid weather no longer threatens Vermont, Andy Rice arrives to relieve Margery's sheep of their wool. "It doesn't hurt a bit, but they are bothered by the indignity," Tasha says.

the curds with a cheese knife, which brandishes blades from several different angles, and stirs them gently with her hands for a long time.

As usual, only experience can tell the cheese-maker when the curds have been sufficiently stirred. "If the cheese squeaks when you bite it, it's ready," Tasha explains. "Pop a curd in your mouth and you'll see what I mean." Curds that have reached the proper degree of squeak-iness are cooled, strained, salted, and seasoned with herbs. Then they are gathered together, swaddled in a cloth, and slipped into the cheese press for a day or so, with fifty pounds of weight applied. When all the whey has been wrung out, the cheese is set out and turned daily for two to three weeks while it forms a tough rind. Finally it is waxed and placed in Tasha's cheese cooler.

Dinner at Corgi Cottage always begins with freshly baked biscuits, which could stand up quite nicely by themselves but become more wonderful still when covered with freshly made butter. Tasha has three or four butter churns at her disposal, but nowadays her preference is for a half-gallon affair that whips up relatively small quantities. She fills it half full of cream and then plunges the dasher up and down for forty-five minutes, until kernels about the size of popcorn form. That's when she dumps the contents into a strainer, flushes out the buttermilk, and places the butter in a big wooden bowl, where it is washed repeatedly and worked with a wooden paddle until every drop of moisture is sweated off. Then comes the artistic part. Tasha wouldn't dream of serving butter that hasn't

been imprinted by a butter mold. She has several to choose from, but the swan mold is her favorite.

TASHA KEPT SHEEP ONCE, WHEN SHE lived in New Hampshire, but she quickly decided to give them up. "I had to get rid of them — they insisted on wandering out and lying on the warm tar road," she explains. "One sheep tried the stunt, and the rest just followed suit. No wonder the public is often likened to sheep." Rather than deal with beasts of low IQ, she obtains "an amplitude of wool" from Seth and his wife, Margery, who keep Romney sheep solely for their long curly fleece. "Every spring the sheep are sheared by Andy Rice, the famed shepherd of Marlboro," Tasha says. "Our small flock scarcely challenges his talents. Andy can easily shear a hundred sheep in a day."

Andy does indeed make shearing, and any other animal-related chore, such as trimming hooves, appear perfectly simple to perform. However, I suspect that these burly animals don't give up their wool quite as easily as his skillful movements make it seem. He flips them on their haunches and goes to work

Newly sheared wool must have the dirt and lanolin washed out before it can be carded. The fleece is combed back and forth into soft rolls called rolags, which will be spun into yarn.

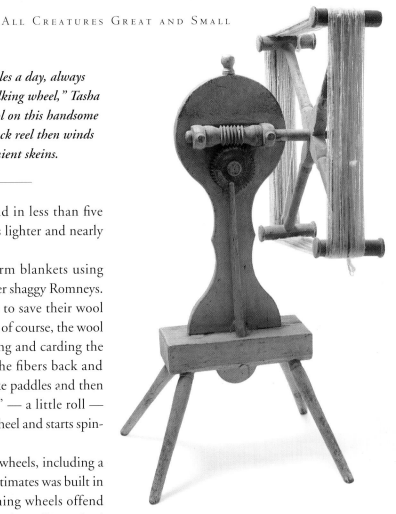

"You can walk several miles a day, always backward, operating the walking wheel," Tasha explains while spinning wool on this handsome piece of machinery. Her clock reel then winds the yarn into convenient skeins.

swiftly with the shears, and in less than five minutes they're ten pounds lighter and nearly naked.

Margery has woven warm blankets using just the fleece shorn from her shaggy Romneys. For her part, Tasha prefers to save their wool for knitting socks. But first, of course, the wool must be spun. After washing and carding the fleece by gently drawing the fibers back and forth over a pair of comblike paddles and then teasing them into a "rolag" — a little roll — Tasha sets up her walking wheel and starts spinning.

Tasha has four spinning wheels, including a walking wheel, which she estimates was built in 1830 or so. "Modern spinning wheels offend the eye," she declares. When the walking wheel has been set up, she starts the huge wheel in motion and paces back and forth, pulling her wool into a long twisted yarn and then reversing the spindle to wind it up. "You can walk twenty miles or more a day while spinning," she'll say over her shoulder while moving the wool back and forth, creating an incredibly even strand.

TASHA GENERALLY HAS SOMEONE ON hand to help with all her many projects. Andy is called in whenever shepherding matters need attention, Kate comes over when the wool is ready for spinning, and Amelia Stauffer often makes the trip from Ohio when soap-making or candle-dipping is in store. Everything in Tasha's life is planned well in advance. In particular, the preparations for soap begin long before the actual event occurs. "These things cannot be accomplished overnight," Tasha declares firmly to anyone who hopes to drop in for an impromptu soap-making session. "First of all, the lard must be thawed. And that takes a good long week."

Tasha gets her lard from Amelia, who has a superfluity. If asked, she will explain patiently that her pig-rearing days are over. "Pigs are just too cunning. My great-grandfather had a tame one who used to ride around town with him in the buggy. It was a sight to behold. And my children tamed a Hampshire once. We named him Martin, and he used to rush around the house. It was all very well and good when he was just a piglet, but he began to wreak some

say), always in the same direction. The goal is a brew the consistency of pea soup, with a lighter color than its original corgi brown. "The way I can tell if it's ready is by holding the spoon up and letting it drip into the cauldron," says Amelia. "When the drips dance on the surface like raindrops on a pond, it's done."

As soon as the soap has reached the proper consistency, it must be poured into a low-sided

box lined with waxed paper and allowed to cool beneath screening, so the greedy corgyn don't attempt to lick it and give themselves impressive stomachaches. It is cut into bars when it's still soft enough to yield to a knife and left to season for several months before use.

Tasha's soap is actually a laundry soap, not a body soap, although it could keep a gardener's hands free of the inevitable stains that soil green thumbs. "Well, it cleans these deplorable hands," Amelia often says. But Tasha prefers to use something milder on her skin. Instead, she whittles shavings of her soap into the wash when she's laundering her aprons and calico frocks.

———

Amelia raises pigs on her farm in Ohio and supplies Tasha with plenty of lard for soap. Accustomed to licking pots clean, the corgyn are kept safely at bay while the two women handle the cauldrons of lye and lard. "It's nasty stuff," Amelia testifies.

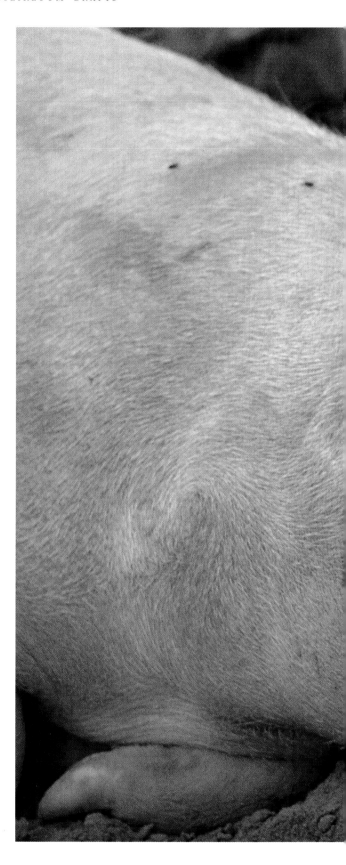

"The most opportune time for making candles is autumn, when the weather is cool, so you can hover over the tripod by the hour without shedding layers," Tasha says while standing and dipping. "Mind your skirts — we don't want anyone going up in flames."

Not all of Tasha's creature-related crafts are connected with farm animals. There's candle-making, for example, which is done with beeswax. Tasha has been fond of bees ever since childhood, when her mother kept them. "Mother had a male friend who wore a very distasteful cologne," she remembers. "No matter where he was in the garden, the bees would find and sting him. I was secretly delighted, of course."

But Tasha's own brush with beekeeping was brief. She didn't have enough fodder to supply honey to keep her bees alive during Vermont's long hard winter, and the supers were far too heavy to be wielded by a beekeeper who weighs less than a hundred pounds. "I lived in the constant fear that I might drop the box and enrage the bees," she explains. So nowadays she orders pure beeswax from an apiary in Michigan and picks up wicks at a local hardware store. Planning ahead, as she always does, she has these supplies in her possession on the day that Amelia comes to help with the candle-dipping.

When candle-making is in the offing, you can smell beeswax and the open fire as you turn into Tasha's meadow, long before you reach the house. The event is usually scheduled for a warm, still autumn day, and Nick has been nurturing that fire for hours. Someone is dispatched to cut willow saplings, and everyone else is busy with scissors in the kitchen, measuring the wicks into sixteen-inch lengths and tying them to the saplings with good strong square knots.

When Tasha dips candles or does anything else, she does it in a big way. The goal is to dip five hundred candles in one day, and the preparations take most of the morning. While we work, plans are laid for workshops and barn dances and accounts of gardens and livestock are shared. Every once in a while, Tasha will sigh and say, "Wasn't that a wonderful tale?" And then she'll coax someone else to launch into another of her favorite stories.

When no fewer than five hundred wicks have been securely tied four inches apart along the saplings, they are taken outside to the cauldron of beeswax melted in water. They are dipped one stick at a time and then hung from sawhorses while the wax cools and hardens a bit. During the first few dunkings, Tasha runs her fingers down the wicks to straighten each one, and that's when the strong knots come in handy. The candles are dipped dozens of times in rotation, while impurities that float to the

surface of the wax are continually strained from the cauldron with a sieve. Slowly the candles gain girth until they are thicker than an inch around. Then they are cooled and stored for a month or so before using.

"Why must they be seasoned?" I ask, just a little impatient to see the candles lit. "Because they burn better," Tasha responds. And it's true. They do give off a fine glow when you light them during the long evenings later in the year. And I've also noticed that in the middle of

Beeswax candles emit the most heavenly scent, especially when the wick has just been snuffed out. All sorts of implements are necessary for lighting up properly, including wick trimmers and candle snuffs. Tasha's trusty pocket knife trims the candles to fit into their holders.

winter, the beeswax gives off a heavenly scent when you snuff out the taper before climbing into bed.

CHAPTER FOUR

A TASTE OF THE PAST

CANNING ❧ OPEN-HEARTH COOKING ❧ CIDER-MAKING

THE KITCHEN IS THE HEART of Tasha's home. It commands a strategic location at the very center of the house, and it's the first room you enter when you arrive. Most people go no further, especially in winter, when the wood-fired cookstove is roaring away. Everyone gathers in the kitchen. Tasha putters about mixing ingredients and stirring broth while a herd of corgyn and cats hover close at hand, begging for scraps. Captain Pegler holds forth in the corner, practicing whatever phrase he has learned in the last hour, and the finches perform their inventory of tweets and trills. So there's plenty of good company.

By anyone's definition, the kitchen is Corgi Cottage's most interesting place, fitted with all the equipment necessary to perform any culinary feat Tasha cares to dream up. Of course, we're not speaking of food processors, toasters, microwaves, and their ilk. Tasha has a few choice words to say about all of these electric gadgets. Instead, she keeps a complete inventory of antique cooking utensils close at hand — beaters, sifters, churns, spoons for stirring specific foods, ladles, molds — as well as tins, crocks, and jars for holding grains, nuts, seeds, crackers, and whatnot. Dangling overhead is a healthy complement of useful herbs, such as dill and thyme, tied in bunches. Also hanging from the beams are baskets full of garlic, shallots, and other frequently used members of the allium family. Mixing bowls, colanders, and sieves of every proportion and shape sit on top of the cupboards, providing Minou, Tasha's one-eyed cat, with a comfy place to curl up

when they aren't being used. In fact, Minou has been known to seize the opportunity and settle on top of rising dough, much to Tasha's consternation. To preclude such disasters, the cook has learned to take precautions and lay something quite sharp and forbidding on top of the dough.

The kitchen is a cozy place stenciled with Scandinavian floral borders by Linda Allen and dominated by the cookstove. Tasha is always there in midmorning, with her feet propped up and a book in her hands.

I F YOU ASK TASHA TO DIVULGE THE secrets of something wonderful she served for lunch, she usually quotes from her family receipt book. ("Receipt" is the word she quite clearly prefers when speaking of recipes. According to the dictionary, the pronunciation is valid, if not still commonly used.) This tome is certainly the most fascinating book of knowledge in a house quite generously stocked

with reference volumes on almost every subject. Handwritten and held together by string, it lies conveniently flat on table or countertop. Flour dusts many of the pages, splatters and spills enhance the directions for whisking and rolling, and fingerprints grace the most popular entries. The book is actually an anthology, primarily composed of the cooking wisdom on Tasha's mother's side of the family, with frequent additions from Dady and other incredible cooks whom Tasha has met during her long career. Papers are tucked in, and Tasha adds to it every once in a while. But by now, her favorite dishes are all chronicled somewhere in its confines.

Although the family receipt book is always by her side when Tasha is cooking, she rarely refers to the directions on its pages. She knows her favorite recipes by heart, and she doesn't really measure things by the regulation teaspoon and tablespoon anyway. Instead, she does it by taste — and by instinct, I suspect. When she starts cooking, ingredients are mixed and vegetables are chopped with such rapidity that she could not possibly have taken a moment to ponder the pages of her precious book. And yet I think she would be horror-stricken if it were ever lost.

Whenever Tasha has gathered a crowd of friends to press cider or thread the looms, she always disappears shortly before noon and doesn't return until it's time to announce the midday meal. She claims that the time has come to feed the corgyn their cottage cheese. In

The family receipt book bears evidence of many scrumptious meals. "At present, I'm particularly keen on receipts that utilize plenty of eggs," Tasha calls from the kitchen as she whips up a batch of cookies.

truth, we all know that she's beginning to fuss over luncheon. Of course, the main dishes have been stewing away for several hours, but there are always a few little garnishes that must be prepared at the last minute.

TASHA IS COMFORTABLE WITH HER cooking skills, but she tends to be just a bit elusive about where it all began, for some reason. If you're foolish enough to ask her how she learned to cook, a mischievous smile will play on her lips and she'll respond by saying, "It all started with mud pies." Chances are that's where the tale will end, although once she did let slip that most of her culinary abilities were honed by preparing meals for her older brothers, who had hearty appetites as well as discriminating taste buds. Apparently her family educated her well, because Tasha really is a cook of great repute, and of all the crafts she has mastered, creating a delicious spread is the one she is proudest of. The highest compliment, of course, is to beg for another serving. But try to pay her a direct compliment and she's apt to give most of the credit to her absolutely fresh ingredients — eggs laid that morning, milk squeezed from the goat's udder just hours ago, vegetables picked while the pot was boiling, and herbs gathered on the way from the garden back into the house. For Tasha, one of the garden's primary functions is to fill her table with compliment-worthy repasts.

Since the garden is only fully functional for a few months of the year, during the remainder of the seasons Tasha makes use of the carrots and beets that she has buried in boxes of sand in the root cellar. She eats onions and potatoes from the pantry as well as pumpkins and squash that she has tucked into corners upstairs. "Members of the squash family must be

stored in a warm spot, so they share our living quarters," she explains quite unapologetically when ushering guests into their rooms. She also spends many, many hours canning, freezing, and drying summer's bounty for use during less fruitful times.

Tomatoes and pears are the fruits she most frequently targets for canning. Every year Tasha puts up fifty jars of tomato sauce, peeling the tomatoes, mashing them, and adding garlic, sugar, salt, basil, thyme, and other herbs ("Heavens, it varies every time I make a batch"). Her own garden generally yields enough tomatoes for the purpose, but friends invariably arrive bearing boxes of their own vine-ripened produce.

Friends are more than pleased to bring bushels of tomatoes when canning season arrives, and not a single one goes to waste. The kitchen is filled with the delicious smell of tomato sauce heavily laced with herbs.

Before Tasha can preserve the pear crop, the juicy fruit must be ripened to just the right degree of softness. Because the season isn't long enough for the pears to soften on the tree, Tasha picks them unripe and places them in boxes upstairs, so guests must make their way through a maze of fruit when journeying to bed for the night. When the pears have turned from rock solid to slightly soft and acquired a

mouth-watering scent, she peels a batch and puts them in a kettle, makes a syrup of salt and sugar, pours the boiling syrup over the fruit, and lets it simmer for twenty minutes. Then she cools the mixture slightly and seals both pears and syrup in jars.

LIKE MANY NEW ENGLANDERS, TASHA has a taste for berries, and she wouldn't think of letting a single one go to waste. Apparently the corgyn have developed a similar appreciation, and they do a splendid job of cleaning up any berries within their reach. Fortunately, plenty remain to be made into raspberry pies and strawberry jam. And enough blueberries elude the ravages of the greedy little

creatures to be frozen or dried for Tasha's famed muffins.

Always resourceful and forever unwilling to let a single piece of produce go to waste, Tasha dries apples and freezes peas, beans, corn, broccoli, and lima beans. She also dries corn in the big antique contraption that fits on the top of the woodstove. The woodstove always seems to be laboring, no matter how hot it happens to be outside.

Tasha insists that everything tastes better when cooked on her woodstove. "Actually, the same receipt prepared in precisely the same way will acquire a totally unique taste depending on where it is cooked," she says. "It's like children in a family — they're all raised by the same parents, but they all turn out quite differently, don't they?" Since she uses the wood cookstove often, she has its temperament down to a fine science. "They're all so eccentric," she muses. "You have to know and respect their hot spots and cool zones. It isn't as simple as it looks." To tell the truth, it doesn't seem simple in the least, and no one but Tasha attempts to touch that finicky piece of cast iron.

HOWEVER, IF YOU'RE VERY FORTU-nate and have braved the driveway in the dead of winter, you arrive to find a fire sputtering in the open hearth with a cauldron of soup suspended by a chain hanging over it. In my opinion, that soup surpasses the woodstove version. But then, appetites are always hardiest after a harrowing winter's journey.

The fireplace also boasts a brick oven built into its masonry, and Tasha occasionally bakes bread or beans inside. First she lights a fire, using twigs scavenged from the woods, and allows its embers to burn out before she removes the ashes. Then she waits for the bricks to cool slightly — "I scatter flour inside. If it scorches, then the bricks are certainly too hot" — before slipping in whatever she plans to bake. Generally, she has an inventory of delectables lined up to go in one after the other, because the oven remains sufficiently warm for two days' worth of intensive baking.

Tasha's breads are legendary. When she was only sixteen, she won her first blue ribbon for her bread, at the Danbury Fair. "I was so

An accomplished cook as well as a weaver, Kate Smith rakes some glowing coals out of the open hearth, places the Dutch oven on a trivet above them, sets a pie inside, and closes the lid. In an hour or so, the pie will be ready to eat.

Although plenty of young friends and relatives are happy to lend a hand when cider is being pressed, Tasha insists on taking a turn at the crank herself. "I'm certain that I can equal my grandson in stamina," she confides while tightening the press.

proud, having outdone all the older ladies in the competition," she still boasts. Once or twice I've managed to witness bits and pieces of the procedure of rolling, kneading, and form-ing the dough into loaves without being sent away on some mission or other. The entire or-chestration is performed with lightning-quick movements on her marble-topped counter, which is generously dusted with flour and scrubbed energetically between steps before she begins some other course of the meal.

One year Tasha tried growing a field of wheat, just because she wanted to experience the entire process of making bread, from plant-ing seeds to baking the loaves. She sent for seeds of a special soft wheat guaranteed to

thrive in her climate, sowed them in spring, threshed the grain herself, and used the blowing end of a vacuum cleaner to winnow it. She insists that the subsequent bread tasted uncommonly good, and I don't doubt her claim. But Tasha's bread is always delicious. If you tell her so, she replies that it's only because she grinds fresh wheat berries every time she bakes. But I've always suspected that the flavor owes its goodness to herbs.

The kitchen and nearby open hearth are not the only places where Tasha prepares food. When things are destined to be sloshed or churned or otherwise splattered about, she much prefers that the task be carried out in less heavily trafficked places. In particular, cider is made outside on the terrace, not far from the barn.

Cider-pressing is an eagerly anticipated annual autumn event. Long before the day of the deed, the attendant machinery must be fetched from storage. Hidden in the recesses of Tasha's house, stashed here and there in the structure's many nooks, is an arsenal of contraptions that perform very specific tasks and are called into service only in certain seasons, depending on their function. The cider press is one such gadget. Composed of several wrought-iron gears, a hopper, and a wooden bucket with open slats, it spends most of the year stored in the barn. However, when autumn arrives, the cobwebs are dusted off, the parts are fitted together, and Winslow is called over to handle the crank.

Besides being tall and courtly and having a fine resonant voice, Winslow possesses considerable strength in his arms. With his help, bushels of Rowan, McIntosh, and Red Delicious apples are carted over from a neighbor's orchard, ground into mash, and then pressed until their juice spills down the grooves in the block of wood below. This process is repeated over and over again, while friends carry the leftover peelings to the compost heap. Meanwhile, several dozen gallon jugs are filled with the apples' nectar, to be served for weeks and handed out to fortunate friends and visitors. Tasha herself is not such a keen consumer. "When I was a child," she explains, "a whole barrel full of cider sat in the cellar, and cider accompanied every meal we sat down to all winter long."

O F ALL THE HOLIDAYS, CHRISTMAS is definitely Tasha's favorite. After all, that is when her culinary talents really come into play. Finally she has a valid excuse to roast a turkey in the "tin kitchen," which fits in front of the open hearth. This piece of equipment, also known as a reflector oven, comprises a curved shiny surface, a spit, and a crank. The bird is stuffed, trussed, and basted with herb butter before being skewered onto the spit and placed in the oven for approximately five hours of rotating. All the while, corgyn and cats are kept at bay and the house is filled with a heavenly scent.

Although the bird is fixed with much fan-

The reflector oven is fitted with a door so the cook can keep track of the bird's progress as it slowly bakes. Porringers catch the grease before it can tempt the corgyn.

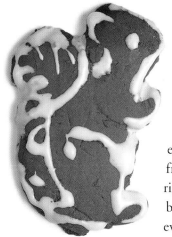

fare, Tasha's favorite part of Christmas is not the main dish but the desserts. Every year she tries something different, to everyone's delight. There are more fruit pies and upside-down and right-side-up cakes than all assembled can possibly consume. After everyone has finished the formal meal, there are candies. The Christmas tree is heavily laden with cornucopias made of decorated paper tied on the boughs with ribbons. Each one is filled to the brim with homemade goodies, and every year Tasha lays plans for those fillings far in advance of Christmas Day. She has cooked up cherry bonbons, chocolate peppermints, and taffy. She has prepared fudge, pralines, caramels, and cookies of all types and tastes. Tasha does nothing by halves.

As you can imagine, the Christmas tree is a resplendent affair. Not only does Tasha make cornucopias, candles, and decorated eggs to adorn it; she also bakes oversize gingerbread cookies, decorates them with frosting, attaches ribbons to their crowns, and suspends them from the tree. She never makes any claims about the edibility of these particular cookies ("The gingerbread has to be very stiff to withstand being suspended for the entire holiday"), but she is extremely proud of the artistry with which she has etched the frosting. In fact, one of Lyndon Johnson's daughters took one look at these ornaments and asked that a few be sent to the White House for the family tree. Of course Tasha obliged.

For the artist, decorating gingerbread is half the fun of making it. Tasha fills paper funnels with icing and then snips the end of the cone so she can apply the topping with absolute accuracy.

just the right tension, as if she had been sitting at the loom herself. In addition, Kate keeps a loom or two of her own in Tasha's barn, just in case there's a dull moment.

The autumn call from Tasha doesn't really come as a surprise — there's been plenty of warning. The sheep have been relieved of their wool many months before; shearing is traditionally done in the spring, long before the hot weather arrives. In the weeks that intervene, the fleece is carded, spun, washed in Tasha's rather potent laundry soap, and scoured until all its natural grease and oil has been removed. Then, as the plumes of goldenrod begin to color up, Tasha mordants the skeins — that is, prepares them to take the dye — by simmering them for an hour in three ounces of alum and one ounce of cream of tartar per pound of wool (the cream of tartar keeps the fibers soft). Thus prepared, the wool is bundled in damp towels and allowed to sit for three days in anticipation of Kate's arrival. By the time Kate comes up the driveway, not only is the wool ready and waiting, but the goldenrod has been freshly harvested.

This wildflower is a welcome volunteer in Tasha's meadow, furnishing a last hurrah long after the daisies and lupines have faded. It far surpasses other people's patches of goldenrod, towering several inches above Tasha's head and forming fine feathery plumes of canary-colored blossoms. There's enough so that Tasha can easily scythe several bushels and still have plenty to admire.

To make dye, it is best to harvest the flowers when they are just beginning to open. Tasha doesn't always achieve that goal, but she does her best. Also in the interest of capturing the best color, she sends Steve out to scythe in midmorning, when the dew has just burned off. He usually takes the opportunity to cut down the entire stalk, but the flowers are all that are needed for the dye pot. The foliage might muddy the soft, clear yellow that the dyers are trying to achieve.

WHEN THREE BUSHEL BASKETS OF goldenrod blossoms have been acquired, the dyers are ready to go into action. Before receiving its stain, the wool must be rinsed thoroughly to remove any traces of the mordant. "If any remains, it's likely to interfere with the color lake," Kate warns. For that purpose, Tasha has been soaking the wool in her enormous wooden tubs for several days. Not one to waste a moment in idleness, Kate builds a crackling fire beneath the tripod and simmers the goldenrod tops in the brass kettle while the wool is being rinsed. She then strains the plant material and places the wool in the kettle, where it is allowed to simmer in the tinted water for an hour. By the time Kate and Tasha begin fishing the skeins out with sticks, they have been transformed to a truly handsome shade of yellow.

Tasha also uses goldenrod to help produce other colors. For instance, sometimes she dyes a few skeins of wool in the goldenrod and then

The meadow that greets your arrival at Tasha's house has many faces. It opens with lupines and spends midsummer blanketed in oxeye daisies. By autumn, goldenrod dominates, until Steve Davie arrives with his scythe.

overdyes them with indigo to achieve a riotous Martian green. More often, however, she uses the indigo vat to procure a stunning royal blue. She is quite proud of her stash of indigo. Many years ago, she acquired quite a quantity for a song, and she still has a generous portion of it. That might be due to the fact that indigo is dissolved in a unique solution. For several weeks prior to dyeing, Tasha politely asks everyone on the property to save their urine. "Margery's boys are delighted to contribute, and the collection is kept in the barn, downwind from

Every hint of the mordant must be rinsed out before wool can be dyed, and for that purpose Tasha readies a couple of huge tubs and her homemade laundry soap. Then the dyers roll up their sleeves and scrub.

pedestrian traffic," she explains. "We need twenty gallons for our purpose, and it should be slightly fermented to do the trick. But that isn't difficult to achieve. After a week, it ripens to a fine swill."

Tasha and Kate use dyes of several different shades while they have the tripod fixed and the cauldron boiling. Since cochineal gives Tasha's petticoats their riveting red color, she dips several skeins in that pot.

When the time to dye comes around, the indigo is dissolved in the urine; when it forms an impressive scum on the surface, the brew is ready to be used as a dye. The wool is allowed to soak for several minutes while it turns a greenish hue. Then the skeins are fished out — rather gingerly, to avoid splashing — and that's when the real drama transpires. "It's like a feat of magic!" Tasha exclaims. The moment the wool hits the air, the color oxidizes and the skeins abruptly become a luscious shade of blue. Repeated dippings darken the color, so the wool is dunked half a dozen times, spending ten minutes in the dye vat and ten minutes in the air each time, until Tasha has obtained the cobalt she is striving for. Bright though it might be, it's the sort of color Ver-

Hanging proudly on Tasha's porch, the skeins present a handsome picture. From left to right, they owe their hues to black walnut, goldenrod, goldenrod and indigo, madder, cochineal, cutch, and indigo.

monters favor, and Tasha has produced innumerable blankets in varying patterns of cobalt and white.

While she was buying her indigo, Tasha also purchased a generous inventory of cochineal for ten dollars a pound, and she's particularly proud of that little bit of forethought: "I felt that fee was rather steep. Well, it's now a hundred dollars a pound, and I'm very pleased that I needn't purchase any further supplies at that outrageous price." Cochineal powder is made from the bodies of a blush-colored tropical insect that is now quite rare, which explains why its value has skyrocketed. It yields a very clear red, just the kind of shade to which Tasha is partial. In fact, cochineal red is the color Tasha traditionally uses for her "good stiff petticoats," so she tints several skeins simultaneously. And she often uses tin as a mordant to make her brilliant undergarments brighter still. "Tin produces an incredibly bright color," she tells me, "but it's terribly poisonous, and I worry about my pets. Of course, I keep the bath under a tight lid."

WHILE THE POTS ARE BOILING, the dyers also prepare colors made from other natural substances. Kate grows dyer's rocket, or weld, especially for the purpose ("Half a bushel of green weld per pound of wool should do the trick," she notes). A vat is also devoted to onion skins from Tasha's vegetable garden, which dye the wool a brassy yellow. But since the severe

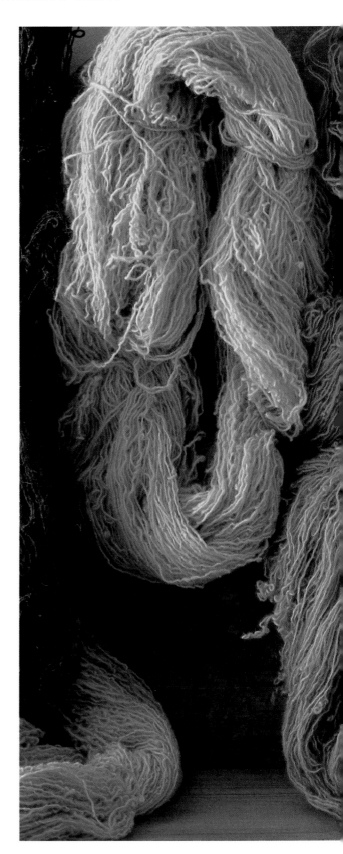

weather in Tasha's neck of the woods prevents her from growing many of the necessary plants, the remainder of the dyes come from afar. Shaking her head and lamenting that "dyemakers up north have a hard go of it, to be sure," Kate explains that she sends for her supply of madder from the south, since *Rubia tinctorum* cannot grow enough roots in northern New England to infuse a dye pot. And cutch *(Acacia catechu)*, a tree native to Pakistan and Burma that produces a rusty shade of brown, is also purchased commercially.

A source from closer afield is the gentleman from upstate New York who delivers Tasha's winter supply of alfalfa hay. He always brings a generous bag of freshly gathered black wal-

Depending on how many times the wool is dunked, indigo deepens from powder blue to midnight blue, providing a variety of shades. Most of Tasha's blankets, especially this jacquard weave, combine indigo with white.

nuts as well, which he gives Tasha in exchange for a piece of pie. Wool requires no mordant to accept the deep brown dye of black walnuts, but Tasha and Kate prepare the dye bath in an iron kettle, trusting that any rust will go into the solution and act as a fixative. "All the dyes we use, with the exception of the onion skins, hold fast and don't fade with time," Kate ex-

plains when asked about her selection of natural materials. "Most plants produce some sort of dye, but few are fast."

FOR WEEKS AFTER THE WOOL HAS BEEN dipped in the dye pots, Tasha's porch is proudly draped with brilliant skeins left to dry and be admired by guests. "Then I wash them all, starting with the lightest colors first, to make certain they hold their colors," Tasha says. "I'm pleased to report that they all come through triumphantly."

After the tinted skeins have undergone their trials by sun and water, they are ready to be woven into cloth. If you're fortunate enough to be invited to spend the night at Tasha's, you'll be given a choice among several guest rooms. My favorite is the downstairs alcove, not far from the warmth of the kitchen cookstove, where the bed snuggles up to a huge old loom. Actually, this loom is one of seven set up in the downstairs rooms. Only three are Tasha's; the rest belong to friends who do not have enough space to accommodate them. However, as you might guess, not a single loom just sits there looking picturesque. They are all warped and hold projects in varying stages of completeness. "With so many looms going simultaneously, I should devote every Sunday solely to weaving, but I haven't achieved that goal to date," Tasha often says, hastening to assure me that "sooner or later, all the projects will get done."

A loom close to the open hearth is always threaded with a modest plaid so Tasha's sons and grandsons can wear handwoven shirts. The boys put plenty of wear on their garments, "but the shirts last for decades."

IN ADDITION TO THE LOOMS SCATTERED throughout Tasha's home, there are some in the barn, which she generally uses only during warm weather. She prefers to keep her favorite looms close at hand, so she can weave whenever a spare moment presents itself. When a pot is simmering on the stove or an artistic idea is hatching in her mind's eye, Tasha often slips off her shoes, sits down at the loom, and manipulates the closely set treadles with her stocking feet. Very often in the twilight of the day you hear the steady clacking of the treadles, punctuated by the rhythmic thumping of the beater being pressed against the weft as she works.

"Weaving goes like lightning compared to the preparation process," Tasha explains to anyone who thinks that weaving must be boring. Because she is an artist, she welcomes the challenge of textile design. "I prefer solid colors myself, but the boys favor checks for their shirting," she tells me, so when the time comes to select a design, she sometimes turns to the well-worn pattern book that sits not far from the loom. More often than not, though, she creates her own. "I can't add two and two, but I can do a splendid weaver's draft," she says. This is simply a piece of paper on which battalions of little X's march back and forth across a grid. The draft might not look like much, but it's actually Tasha's battle plan. When she begins a project, it tells her which colors to thread through the heddles for the warp. As time wears on, it becomes progressively tattered and creased as she consults the X's to determine how to choreograph the shuttles as she throws them back and forth, forming the fill. For the duration of the project, that modest piece of paper is every bit as important to Tasha as the family receipt book.

After she has decided on a design, the loom must be warped. The dressing of her looms is an event that requires the talents of several weaving friends, who gladly get together to

make quick work of the task. Tasha dotes on these occasions. She puts the crowd up in various nooks and crannies of the house, reward-

Although Tasha has tried her hand at overshot weaving, she says the pattern is "a little too dizzying" for her taste. She has also tried tartans, but she prefers simple plaids by far.

ing their efforts with incredible meals while the work is in progress and a boisterous barn dance when it is finished.

MEANWHILE, THERE'S ALL SORTS of action at the spool rack (or skarne, as Kate calls it), as dozens of spools feed yarn onto a warping board of such impressive dimensions that its pegs are swiftly wound with fifteen- and twenty-yard-long warps. "Its beauty lies in its simplicity," Kate always says when I express awe at this process. Not only must yarns of the proper colors be wound back and forth enough times to achieve the precise length, but they must all remain in their assigned positions when the weavers take the warp off the board and transfer it to the loom. Tasha assures me that the weaver's cross, which is tied with brightly colored string, keeps everything in the correct order. "You have to be ever so careful, though," she cautions. "If you lost the weaver's cross, it would be very bad news indeed." That has never happened to her. Somehow, all those threads (and Tasha often navigates warps that are more than a thousand strands wide) are taken down, crocheted into a chain, and carried to the loom without becoming hopelessly entangled. But there's always the potential for disaster, and that's part of the excitement.

Before she met Kate, Tasha patiently dressed each loom thread by thread, "but Kate shared with me many eighteenth-century shortcuts, like how to thread five or six strands through the heddles simultaneously. It saves so much time and agony."

In jest, Tasha frets that if she sits at one task for too long she'll be afflicted by a spreading of the hips, which she refers to as "weaver's bottom." "I have to move around," she protests if someone offers to save her from rising by fetch-

The beauty of linen is that its texture grows silkier and softer with time. "Flax doesn't accept a dye, but the years deepen the color," Kate explains. On one vintage piece of linen, the weaver signed his work in oak gall.

I wear linen undergarments. I simply prefer the feel of this fabric," she declares whenever anyone questions the prudence of weaving fifteen yards of the world's most stubborn fiber.

GRANTED, SHE HAS HAD PLENTY OF practice, starting with the homegrown flax she harvested, dyed, and wove into cloth for her brother's shirt. She knows just how to discipline the fibers. Her weave is as tight and fine as you can imagine, and the finished product feels like silk. But progress is slow, even in her experienced hands. "When the piece is completed, washed, and hung to dry, that is a proud moment in my life," she admits.

Meanwhile, the brilliant red wool that Tasha uses for the outer portion of the petticoats is being woven comparatively swiftly on a loom in the barn. "I can weave a yard of wool in an hour," she points out. As soon as the fabrics are ready, she places them together, pads them with lamb's wool, and quilts them. "And they will be very snug indeed — you can count on it," she says. When Tasha receives inquiries about how she remains warm throughout the long Vermont winters, she always gives full credit to her quilted wool petticoats: "They do the job admirably, and I just add layers as the thermometer drops."

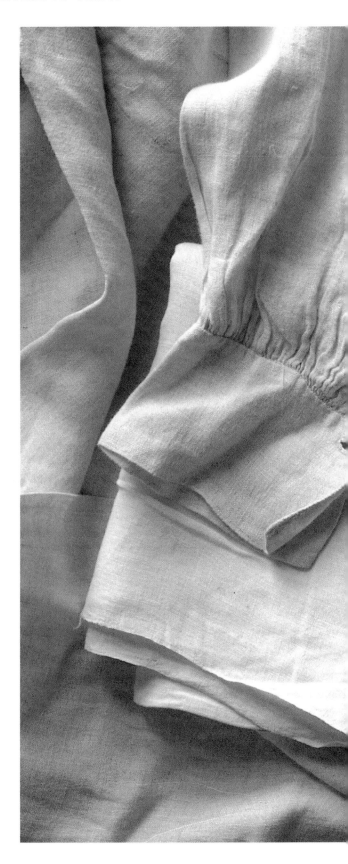

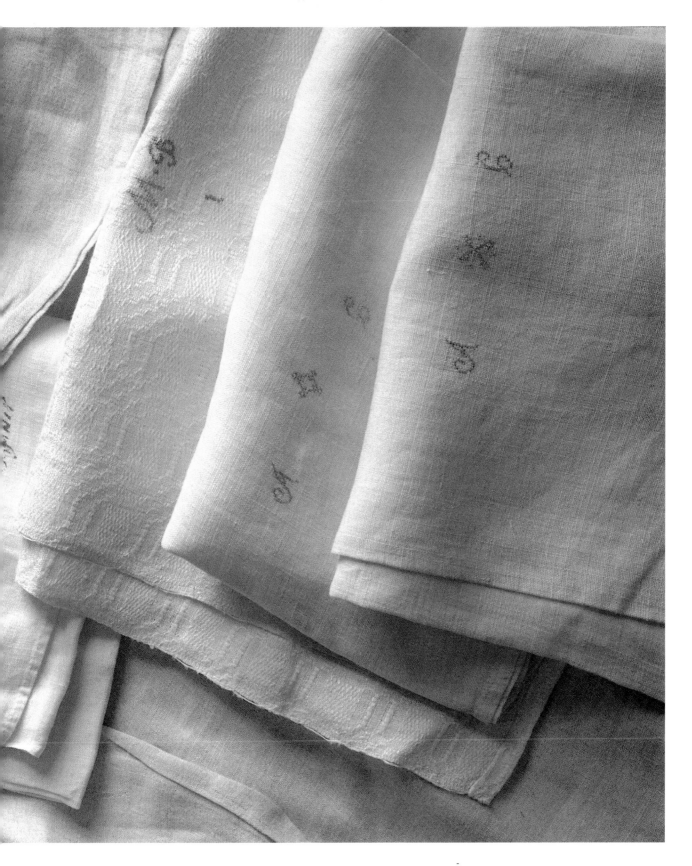

CHAPTER SIX

A STITCH IN TIME

QUILTING ∾ LACE-MAKING ∾ SEWING

O F ALL HER CRAFTS, TASHA IS fondest by far of those that she can accomplish when sitting quietly beside the fire in the evening. "Only daylight will do for watercolors," she says, so as soon as the sun sets she puts down her paints, and quite often she takes up a needle instead.

The beauty of sewing is that it requires few tools beyond the skill of the seamstress. With a pair of dainty scissors, a needle, some thread in varying shades (Tasha sometimes refers to it as "twist," following Beatrix Potter's lead in *The Tailor of Gloucester*), a little beeswax to help the needle glide, a box full of pins, and perhaps a measuring tape, she is all set to undertake an evening's work.

Whenever Tasha reaches for needle and thread, she always slips on a gold thimble that has her initials engraved in its surface. "Every proper young lady received a gold thimble on her eighteenth birthday," she tells me, in the bewildered tone that she uses only when I have failed to recognize one of the essential facts of life. "My mother's thimble became so worn from constant use that a perilous hole appeared in its tip."

At any given moment, Tasha is deeply involved in several sewing projects. Some are long-term affairs; for instance, I have heard her declare with considerable resolution, "Before I leave this earth, I intend to finish my quilt — you can count on it." She can't recall exactly when she began work on the quilt, but it has definitely been more than a decade since she cut out the squares. "The pattern is called Yan-

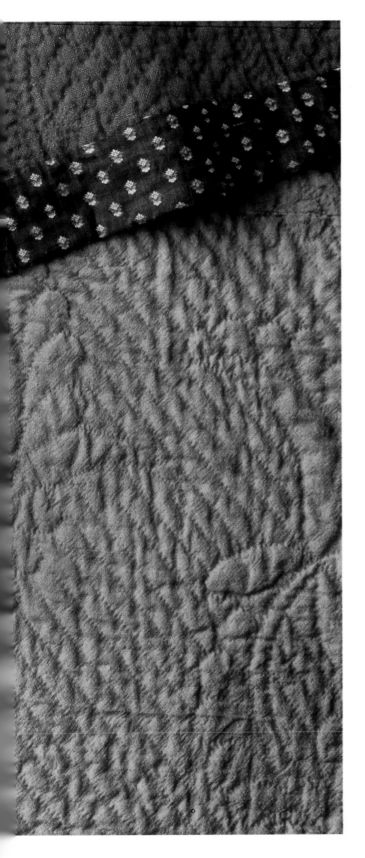

kee Pride, so I thought the theme was certainly appropriate," she explains, "and I'm pleased to report that it's finally reached the piecing-together stage."

SOME OF TASHA'S ONGOING PROJECTS are packed away waiting for her interest to be rekindled, but she does plenty of handiwork on a daily basis. She tackles the mending, for example, with particular urgency. Few tasks provide Tasha with greater pleasure than giving a tattered garment a new lease on life. "Look at this," she says proudly while lifting her skirts ever so slightly. "I've darned all my wool stockings, and they'll now serve me several more winters." Of course, the stockings are called into service only from autumn until mid-spring. As soon as the ground warms up enough to plant corn, Tasha goes barefoot.

Instead of using a wooden darning egg, Tasha employs a miniature bottle gourd to keep the surfaces of her stockings separate. "Oh, it's an old New England trick," she insists. "I'm certain that I didn't discover it singlehandedly."

Although Corgi Cottage is comfortably warm by day, Tasha likes to let it become "cold enough at night to make forced bulbs content." Quilts wadded with carded fleece between layers of linen and wool keep her warm.

When Tasha knits her Nordic socks, five double-pointed needles ensure that they are perfectly seamless. "I have a whole basket of needles of every gauge and every description," she says.

Not only does the gourd have a rounded body of just the right size to fit easily in a sock, but it also boasts a six-inch neck to simplify insertion and retrieval.

Stockings are not the only pieces of apparel that require occasional repair. Tasha's favorite dresses and aprons see continual wear, and you can just imagine the rigors that face the master gardener's clothes. Quite literally, they go through the wringer on a regular basis. Although they are all well lined and constructed of the sturdiest goods, they inevitably become threadbare in spots. Yet Tasha hates to part with a beloved dress, so she forestalls that moment by applying her needle diligently. She keeps a supply of embroidery thread in cotton and wool just for the purpose, as well as a fine stock of darning needles in all sizes.

Knitting needles are also called into service for repair as well as construction. Tasha learned to knit from her Scottish nanny, who was renowned for her ability. "Of course, I'm not endowed with her skill by any means. I can't even do cables," Tasha protests when compliments are sent her way. But when it comes to knitting and purling, she can certainly click away with the best of them, and she has a fine repertoire of fancy stitches as well. When her children were young, she knit all sorts of sweaters and scarves for them, and the many shawls that lie at hand around the house are also her handiwork.

These days, Tasha's favorite knitting projects by far are socks and mittens, intricately patterned pieces that are usually meant as gifts for very special friends. She favors the Nordic patterns she learned from her talented friend Linda Allen, which are usually so complex that she must lay them out on graph paper first. "Linda worked on the wrong side," Tasha explains, "but I operate on the right side instead." For several months before Christmas, you're bound to find her sitting by the fire in the evening, working on a bulky pair of socks or mittens. "I want my friends to have toasty fingers and toes — that's essential," she says. Tasha enjoys repairing mittens and socks almost as much as she likes making them. In fact, she is very pleased to see that someone has worn a hole in her gift. "I just unravel the foot and put in a new one," she explains while seeing

Tasha's sewing basket includes a bodkin for running ribbon through lace, embroidery scissors, a thread winder, thimbles, packages of needles, a tape measure, dainty buttons from her great-grandmother, and a stiletto for doing white work.

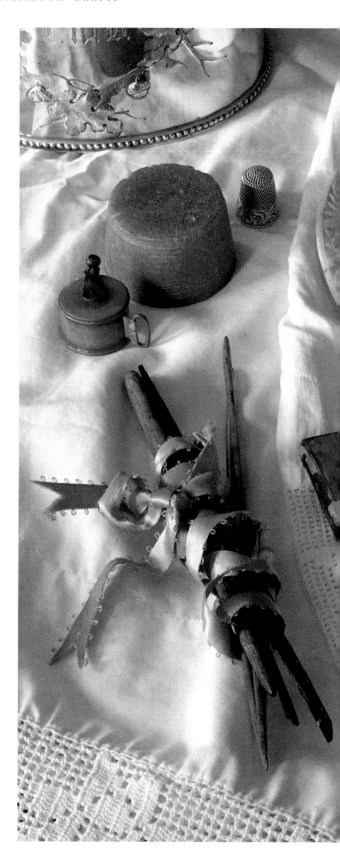

to a pair of Winslow's boot socks. "It's a snap, really."

The knitting needles also materialize when Tasha is making lace, although she uses much smaller needles than those she wields for the Nordic projects. Beside her favorite chair sits a frequently consulted copy of *Classic Knitted Cotton Edgings*, with several bookmarks tucked between the pages. Without exception, Tasha's pillowcases and petticoats have a frill of knitted lace adorning their hems.

ALTHOUGH TASHA HAS NEVER EM-broidered or crocheted white work, she greatly admires those crafts. Her bureau is filled with carefully folded handmade lace collars, lace shawls, and pelerines to dress up her clothes if the occasion warrants an extra frill. Just in case she might feel compelled to add white work to her long roster of skills, a collection of highly intricate vintage lace-pricking patterns waits in readiness. And if she someday decides to master bobbin lacemaking, she can always call on her friend Joan DeGusto for help.

Ask Joan a question about the clothing of any era and she is likely to know the answer. Not only does she possess an encyclopedic knowledge of attire throughout the ages, from crinolines to bonnets, but she can sew up any style you like in a flash. Since she shares Tasha's interest in vintage clothing, she comes to Corgi Cottage frequently, always bringing some sewing to keep her hands busy while she visits.

Tasha believes that everyone has an era with which they identify. Joan harbors an affinity for the first decade of the twentieth century, with its pigeon-breasted bodices and slender skirts. Tasha hearkens further back. Everything she loves, from her looms to her cooking utensils, comes from the 1830s. She will tell you that

she was busy making replicas of clothes from that era before she actually studied a single original dress. "It's uncanny. I just have an innate sense for the styles of those times. That's why I feel certain that I must have once been on this earth in 1830," she says matter-of-factly.

Tasha definitely seems most comfortable in the long skirts and fitted bodices of the 1830s. She has nothing complimentary to say about modern fashions. "Total abominations, that's what they are," she proclaims with considerable fervor. And when she spies a woman in pants, she whispers, "Why would a lady want to parade around in men's clothing? Trousers are perfectly fine for gentlemen, but they don't enhance a female figure in the least."

On a daily basis, Tasha wears simple handmade frocks with fitted bodices, set-in waist-

---

"They knew how to be frugal," Tasha says approvingly of the ladies who traced her antique pricking patterns. "They copied them on the backs of letters."

Recalling the trials of recreating an 1870s dress, Tasha says, "Oh, it was very complex indeed, with lots of detail work and piping and a watchpocket as well." A bustle adds "back interest."

remembers. "She was perfectly beautiful in appearance, and she stitched her own coming-out dress. All the other girls were envious and begged for similar frocks, so she got out her needle and gold thimble to earn a bit of money from her talents." In particular, Tasha learned to smock by watching her mother pull threads of yarn patiently through muslin to make intricately smocked shepherd's shirts for her brother. "All the while, as she was working, she would tell me about how the smocking in the men's shirts was particular to their occupations, so when they went to fairs, they could guess one another's work by what kind of embroidery they had on their chests."

AT THE MOMENT, TASHA IS INORDInately fond of a style she has dubbed "the Stillwater dress." When her crafts-oriented friends began convening on a regular basis to warp the loom or dip candles, her sons started referring to these talented followers as "the Stillwater movement." "And I'm the eldress," Tasha says proudly. Since no one

dares to show up at Tasha's in jeans, the women needed appropriate attire for the elaborate barn dances Tasha stages. She offered to design a dress that might fit everyone's taste and figure and yet provide ample room for unencumbered movement. That was when the Stillwater dress was born. It boasts a full skirt, wide sleeves, and cartridging at the midriff to soften the lines into the waist. Tasha's version is made of light Austrian wool with piping at the armholes and waistband.

Tasha's day dresses are one thing, but her evening wear is another matter entirely. "Her sewing expertise is phenomenal," Joan says, sighing in admiration. Just for a lark, Tasha will study an old garment from top to bottom and then reproduce it exactly. "I never, ever take a dress apart to make a pattern!" she says with a tinge of horror. Amazing though it seems, she needs only to examine a garment carefully inside and out to copy it. "I cut a pattern from muslin and then perfect the fit by draping it over my lay figure," she explains. Although others call their dress forms dummies, Tasha refers to hers as a lay figure, and of course it has a name: Aida.

Depending on the project at hand, Aida is clothed in bodices ranging in style from Sévigné to Circassienne, with high waists, fitted waists, or stomachers and layers of folds falling

Originally adults' gowns, these nineteenth-century examples of the dressmaker's craft now fit only young girls.

in every manner typical of the 1830s. "The folds must be tacked onto the lining," Tasha explains as she busily pins Aida. "That's the only way to make them fall properly." Her fingers work efficiently as she pulls yards of fabric into order, coaxing them into form. "And piping is the most important finishing touch,

but mind that you cut it on the bias to avoid puckers. I never bother to purchase expensive cording — grocery string works just dandy to line the piping."

Brushing off expressions of awe by saying, "It all comes from practice — you could easily do it yourself," Tasha makes clothes that are not only incredibly complex to look at but handsome inside as well. "Linings are essential," she says firmly. No matter how elaborate a taffeta or lawn gown might be, its lining is generally cotton, as "cotton gives the garment

strength and body." Of course, the proper underclothes establish the silhouette. "A corset is required for an evening dress," Tasha declares. In the 1830s, stays were laced so tightly that two or three inches vanished from the woman's abdomen and waist while the fullness spilled over the top. "Tasha scarcely needs a corset to decrease her waist size," Joan observes, "but it helps add bulk elsewhere." Tasha insists that in addition to correcting slouching, corsets prevent lower back pain. "Oh, they're perfectly comfortable to wear, just as long as you don't eat," she says.

Beneath the corset lies a chemise with a very becoming scooped neckline that reveals the shoulders to best advantage. And on top are many yards of meticulously tucked, gored, darted, draped, folded, smocked, and otherwise enhanced fabric. In the 1830s, more than a dozen kinds of sleeves were in fashion; Tasha has reproduced each one, though she has a penchant for voluminous gigot, or leg-o'-mutton, sleeves. The bodices vary considerably in detail, but the skirts invariably boast reams of gathered material to accentuate the hourglass shape. Those gathers are masterpieces in themselves. Somehow Tasha smooths the fabric down so

---

One of Tasha's favorite dresses is a simple, feather-light dotted-swiss gown worn first in the 1820s. On her dressing table she keeps a chalk profile of her "three times great" grandmother clad in a similar fashion.

there is never a bulge at the waist but plenty of flattering fullness that drapes gently from the hip down to the floor. The trick lies in cartridging, which is done by lining up rows of running stitches in regimental order.

DEPENDING ON THE SEASON AND Tasha's mood on a given day, her favorite dress might be either the purple print or the black taffeta gown. She puts a great deal of thought into the fabric she selects for each project, often sending abroad if she can't find what she needs closer to home. When she decides to make a replica, she envisions the texture as well as the color and print of the dress. "Tasha likes tiny rose motifs," Joan observes. "After all, she is a Tudor." She prefers vibrant shades, "especially those that don't easily show soil."

Since Tasha's gowns fit snugly and have dozens of tiny buttons in back, donning them is no easy feat. "They must have been acrobats in the 1830s," she mutters as she tries to get into a particularly complicated outfit. More likely, judging from the fine silks and woven cottons of the originals, the women who wore these fashions every day had ladies' maids at their beck and call. Fortunately, when Tasha is putting on her finery for a festive event, several friends are generally close by to lend a hand. And she needs no help with her work clothes. She just slips into her everyday dresses as though they were a second skin. There's no doubt about it, the 1830s become Tasha.

CHAPTER SEVEN

THE WORLD IN MINIATURE

MARIONETTES ❧ TOYS ❧ THE DOLLHOUSE

ESPECIALLY IN THE DEPTHS OF winter, when outdoor recreation is sparse and the garden is slumbering, I often phone Tasha in the evening to find out whether her primrose seeds have germinated or to share a crucial bit of knowledge about the care and feeding of camellias. No matter when I call, she is always deeply immersed in some sort of fruitful endeavor; she believes, as she says, that "idle hands are the devil's playground." Lately, whenever I ring, her hands are preoccupied with making toys. "I'm just working on another owl," she confesses, "but do continue talking — I can keep

right on with my project." And so we discuss the ins and outs of viola propagation or worry about the weather and its effect on the cinnamon pinks while Tasha completes her toy. She invariably provides a running progress report as we speak. "You should see this owl," she says. "He's a dandy. I just sewed on a pair of tiny button eyes, and he's acquired quite a mischievous expression. No doubt he's dreaming of the field mice he plans to pick up."

Tasha never truly left childhood and all its winged dreams behind. If you try to discover the source of her fountain of youth, she calmly explains that her imagination never faded. Her

favorite injunction, often spoken with some impatience, is "Use your imagination!" She is as young at heart as her whimsical illustrations might suggest, and her house is filled with things to play with. Not far from the kitchen is an elaborate multilevel dollhouse with more comforts than her own home. Tasha likes to fuss with it, dreaming up some little luxury for its inanimate inhabitants. Down a long and winding corridor is the marionette theater, complete with a prodigious cast of stringed characters hung on the nearby wall, perpetually anticipating their cue. Seth carved the handsome pews where the audience sits.

L IKE MOST PEOPLE, TASHA BEGAN playing when she was very young. In fact, her earliest memory is of receiving a toy cow as a gift when she was two years old ("My Scottish nanny insisted on cutting off the horns for fear that I would pierce myself," she explains). But most people's affection for toys dwindles with passing years, whereas in Tasha's case, the feeling never faded.

Seth is not a man of many words, but he requires very little prodding to launch into

---

With passing years, the dog that Tasha created of fur and wood for The Bremen Town Musicians *looks increasingly bedraggled. "He's quite convincing, don't you think? He even hangs his head at a pathetic angle."*

lengthy descriptions of the incredibly complex games that his mother invented for the entertainment of her growing family. "She wasn't just humoring us," he assures me. "My mother loves toys, and she especially loves playing with dolls. I'm certain that she enjoyed our games as much as we did."

The first toys were simple wooden farm animals carved for the amusement of the children when they were toddlers. Some still sit on the mantel above Tasha's open hearth. Other vestiges of playtimes past include stuffed magpies, stuffed bunnies, rag dolls, and paper dolls by the ream, with quantities of paper clothes to accompany each creation. Tasha worked long and hard to encourage her family's imagination, and she turned out some incredible examples of toy-making skill, ones that put factory-made playthings

to shame. Occasionally, however, the children were given the ultimate treat of a trip to F.A.O. Schwarz in New York City to select toys.

"Every child had a favorite," Tasha recalls. "Seth found Mert Boggart and fell so deeply in love with him that I had to build a house for him to live in. Mert was a troll, terribly naughty and rather ugly as well. He had a tooth missing in front and green mosslike hair. Efner's special toy was one of her mother's creations, a baby doll that could be bathed. "He was made of bisque fired in a friend's kiln and jointed together with elastic so no harm would come to the business end when he was in the tub," Tasha remembers. "It took a full nine months to craft that doll. When he was complete, we held a baby shower in his honor."

The marionette shows began as entertainment for the children's dolls. Every year the family threw a huge Christmas party, and Tasha felt certain that the dolls were jealous. So she set to work on a puppet show for their holiday diversion. All the children at the nearby school were also invited to attend.

At first Tasha confined the marionette shows to standard and easily staged fairy tales, such as "Little Red Riding Hood" and "Jack and the Beanstalk" ("with a stalk that shot up so lustily that it nearly scraped the ceiling"). One year the family staged "Saint George and the Dragon," for which Seth concocted a slithering monster several yards long. "He was of fire-breathing temperament," Tasha recalls, "so we stuffed a long enema tube down the length of his body. The boys took great pleasure in grinding up charcoal powder to go into a pouch in his throat. When the dragon was called upon to perform, Tom climbed under the stage and blew into the tube, causing an ominous cloud of black smoke to come billowing from his throat."

Long after Tasha's children reached adulthood, she still gave puppet shows. That explains why she asked Seth to build a marionette theater in the alcove adjacent to the barn. It's an

---

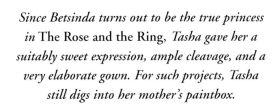

Since Betsinda turns out to be the true princess in The Rose and the Ring, *Tasha gave her a suitably sweet expression, ample cleavage, and a very elaborate gown. For such projects, Tasha still digs into her mother's paintbox.*

"Emma was dying to see Swan Lake, so I made a marionette. It's not exactly the right period for the 1830s," Tasha confesses, "but no matter." Not far away hangs the dashing hero from **The Rose and the Ring,** *Prince Giglio.*

enchanting place of dark wood and resonant echoes, always poised on the brink of reality, with a whole cast of characters waiting to come to life. The forty-three marionettes currently suspended around the stage all have roles in the

same play, Tasha's production of William Makepeace Thackeray's *The Rose and the Ring.* A dozen years ago, she decided that the time had come to do something truly ambitious, so she found a tale with more heroines and villains than anyone can comfortably keep track of and set to work with her friend Linda Allen to make the characters. Most of the puppets have heads and hands that were modeled of clay, cast in plaster of Paris molds, and baked in the oven. The molds are important, because sometimes duplicate characters are called for. As Tasha

Emma and Captain Thaddeus Crane enjoy all manner of comforts and conveniences in their well-appointed dollhouse. Birdcages are in every room, including the kitchen. "Birdsong is a necessity," Tasha proclaims.

---

points out, "You can't change the costume of a marionette." However, she requires the services of only one eight-piece corgi orchestra, "which plays Vivaldi to perfection," and one guest conductor, Pasquale Fellini, an overstuffed cat with a tendency to use his tail as a baton when the tempo picks up.

Tasha's favorite part of the production was undoubtedly making the costumes. Each marionette's clothing is absolutely impeccable in every detail; she used the first edition of Thackeray's fairy tale, which includes his original drawings, as a guide. And she is anxious to begin work on yet another set of marionettes. "I'm itching to make an Ichabod Crane," she admits. In anticipation of a production of *The Legend of Sleepy Hollow,* Seth put in a revolving stage, so the Headless Horseman will appear to gallop at breakneck speed while the scenery whirs past.

I N THE MEANTIME, TASHA BUSIES HERself making gorgeous gowns for Emma, her favorite doll. Emma — named for Tasha's favorite aunt, who generously allowed visiting little girls to play in her memorably elaborate German dollhouse — lives in the dollhouse with Captain Thaddeus Crane, several caged birds, a herd of corgyn, and a Russian wolfhound. You could spend a lifetime engrossed in the miniature world that Tasha has created for these toys.

Tasha wanted a cozy environment for her dolls, so she furnished their house with all the little details that make a place feel like home. In addition to a full complement of stuffed chairs, the parlor contains footstools, several bound classics, little watercolors on the walls, a servant's bell, and family photographs and tiny peacock feathers as mementos. There's a musket over the fireplace, a cello waiting to be played, and a basket of wood by the fire. Beside the bureau and bed in the bedroom are a spinning wheel and a yarn reel, with a tiny handwoven basket of yarn skeins always in readiness.

The dollhouse has three levels, with the kitchen on the ground floor, a feature that Tasha is threatening to change. "It should be higher up," she observes, "because Emma is always working in the kitchen. Maybe I'll put the parlor in the basement instead."

There's plenty to keep Emma occupied in Tasha's doll kitchen. Sitting on the floor are a stoneware butter churn, many crocks, and a basket of kindling ready and waiting to fire the cast-iron cookstove. Hanging on the wall and sitting on the shelves of cupboards are funnels, graters, pans, casseroles, and every other gadget that a good cook might require. There's a bird in a cage by the window to entertain Emma while she wields her tiny rolling pin or washes her yellow pitcher and mixing bowls.

Any resemblance that the dollhouse might bear to Tasha's own home is purely intentional, right down to the tiny renditions of her furniture made by Margery, Seth's wife. Seth explains that creating doll furniture poses the same challenges as crafting full-size reproductions, "except you don't have to worry about anyone leaning back too far on the chairs."

Actually, Captain Thaddeus pre-dates his bride by several years. "He's carved solidly of wood and weighs quite a lot," Tasha notes. For maneuvering ease, he has rounded ball-and-socket joints, just like the wooden figures that artists use as models ("It wasn't easy making those joints with a penknife," Tasha points out). Then the joints were strung with heavy elastic. Emma is "far cleverer in construction"; like her husband's, her arms and legs are carved of wood, but her joints are wired, "which is why she's every bit as supple as a marionette." Her torso is made of kidskin stuffed with lavender. Furthermore, Tasha tucked sprigs of liverwort, lungwort, and bleeding heart in the appropriate places. Emma's head is crafted of Sculpey crowned by a neatly styled mohair wig. Needless to say, there is usually an adoring corgi or two at her feet, undoubtedly begging

for food. Each dog is made of tanned chipmunk skin, "gained from an unfortunate donor killed on the road."

TASHA DOTES ON HAND-SEWING doll clothes, and both Emma and Captain Thaddeus possess very full wardrobes. Captain Thaddeus is fitted with a dashing uniform as well as several well-tailored civilian suits, each complete with starched collar and pocket watch. For her part, Emma dresses with all the modesty befitting a beautiful young lady of the nineteenth century. Every tuck and pleat, from her petticoats to the lace shawls she pins with a tiny brooch, is sewn to perfection and is absolutely authentic to the 1830s. She wears leg-o'-mutton sleeves to accentuate her tiny waist. When she is standing in front of the tiny copper sink pump washing the miniature china or grating carrots at the little food grinder, she wears a starched white apron to keep her frock from getting soiled. Tasha designs Emma's clothes herself, custom-fitting them to the doll's dimensions and using Kleenex or toilet paper to make the pattern. Emma shares Tasha's prejudice against bare elbows, and ever since her much-publicized nuptials (when she and Captain Thaddeus were wed, *Life* magazine featured the event), she has shown no cleavage whatsoever and has kept her finely sculpted shoulders politely hidden beneath lace collars.

Before Emma and Captain Thaddeus set up housekeeping together, they undoubtedly exchanged endearments via Sparrow Post. Ever

When Tasha's children were growing up, their dolls indulged in an ongoing correspondence via Sparrow Post. Every letter was carefully sealed with wax to protect it from prying eyes.

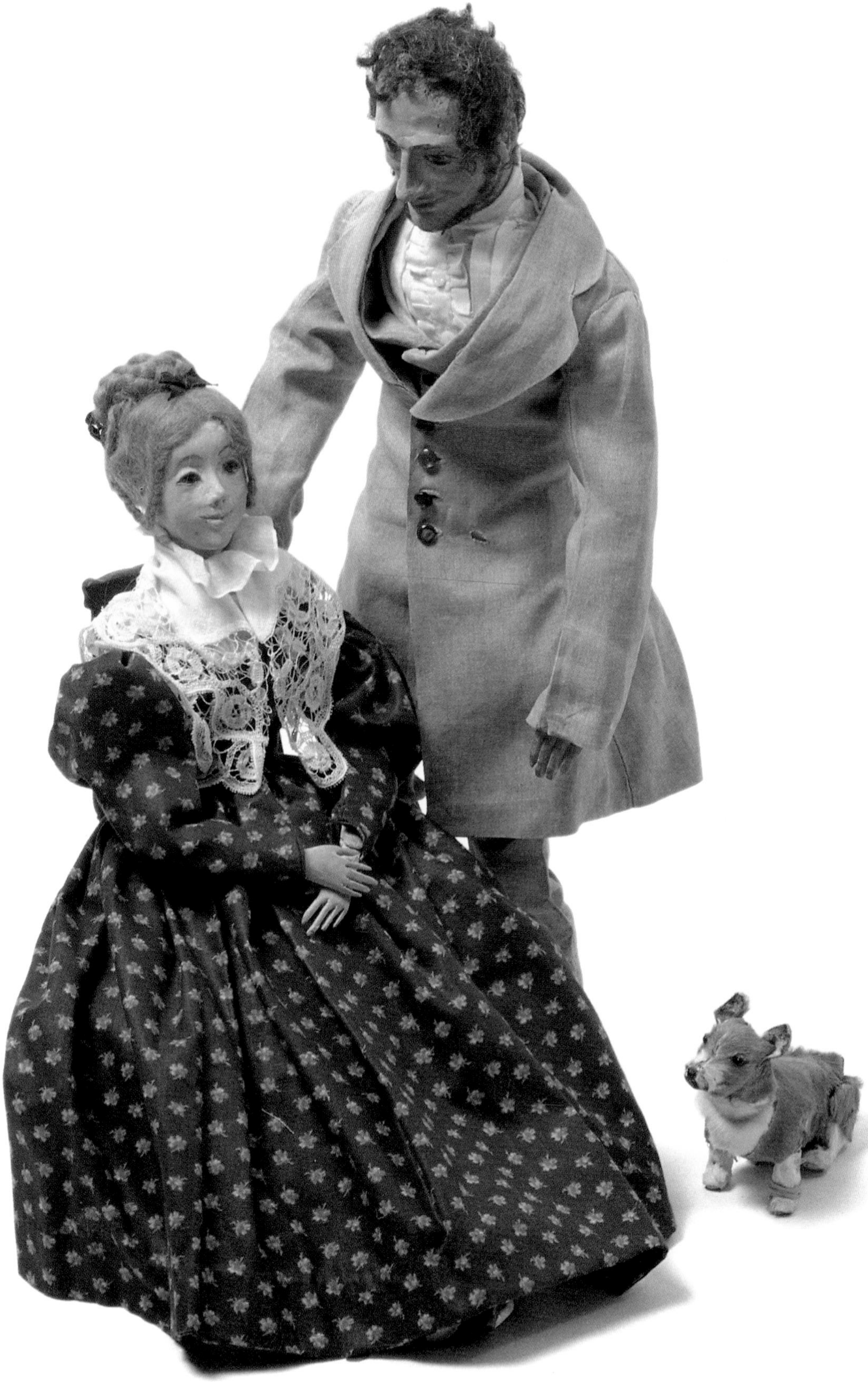

*Tasha always says that she "simply
fell in love with Emma. You've heard the
Pygmalion story, no doubt. Well, that's what
happened when I created Emma."
So it's little wonder that her wardrobe
and accouterments are so
very intricate.*

since Tasha's children were very young, their
toys have corresponded, sending back and
forth minute letters written on tiny stationery
adorned with microscopic illustrations. Each
letter is neatly folded, sealed, and tucked in a
tiny mailbox attached to the front of the dollhouse. "We called it Sparrow Post," Seth recalls, "and we would spend the entire schoolday

anticipating the moment when we could come
home and find a letter addressed to our doll."

On holidays the dolls exchanged greeting
cards, which eventually led to a homemade
book of Valentines, a little contrivance that
Tasha dreamed up because "certain toys had
formed particularly intimate bonds." The
book is a charming publication, only a couple of inches in length and width, yet filled
with intricate advertisements for Valentine
cards rendered in great detail. The fron-
tispiece proclaims its publisher's intentions:
"This catalogue brings you our finest selection of Valentines designed to cover every ro-
mantic situation from the passionate, the
polite, the sentimental, the humorous, to the
bashful."

ASHA'S ORIGINAL BOOK OF VAL-
entines was part of another little diversion that she devised for her children's enjoyment, and probably for her own
amusement as well. Periodically she published
the equally tiny *Mouse Mills Catalogue*, which
pictured and described all manner of toy trinkets and doll clothing in its pages. Over the
years the catalogue became increasingly elaborate, until the dolls could select from petticoats,
gentlemen's nightcaps, jackets, and such con-
ceits as "the French jersey direct from Paris."
That particular item was available in bright
red or "in black for that 'arty' touch." There
were Mouse Mill stockings ("they fit, they
wear, they don't sag") as well as "the best round

*Tasha has made two stuffed crows,
the Reverend Barkadiddy and Edgar Allan
Crow. Close by is Horatio Rabbit, Tasha's first
bunny, made years ago. Like all rabbits,
he has many relatives, including
Wolsey O'Hare, a recent creation.*

garters in red or black." There was "a charming negligee of voile trimmed with lace, just
right for that evening at home," and several
incredibly ornate Victorian fashions for the
well-dressed doll.

Each delightful and humorous description
was followed by a price in buttons — in the
case of the more ornate items, quite a large

number. Of course, Tasha's children were very anxious to acquire quantities of this unique form of tender. To help bolster their coffers, they received buttons in payment for their chores, "but they also asked the neighbors if they had any excess buttons lying around to donate to a worthy cause. As a result, I have a splendid button collection," Tasha says with a twinkle in her eye.

As long as the children could come up with the requisite number of buttons, they were free to order whatever they liked from the catalogue. "My mother always produced whatever she advertised," Seth substantiates. Some projects took longer to produce than others, but the catalogue explained that to its customers in its terms of sale: "We will do our best to fill orders as promptly as possible, but beg your patience for delays." It also included further instructions to avoid disappointment: "When

"You should see my goat," Tasha says with undisguised pride. "She's got a fine form, a nice straight back, and a very pliable udder. Furthermore, she gets into no mischief."

ordering, be sure to give careful measurements and sizes. State colors too." Those words of guidance were signed by the proprietor of Mouse Mills, Timothy D. Mouse. "It was great fun and we carried it on for years," Tasha recalls as she rewraps each tiny catalogue in tissue and packs them all back in their basket for safe-keeping.

TODAY THE SPARROW POST box might not be as stuffed with correspondence as it was when the Tudor children were young, but Tasha is still deeply immersed in toys. At present, soft toy animals have her undivided attention. Screech owls are her favorite creations by far, and she is continually increasing the flock. By anyone's standards, they are absolutely beguiling. All have tufted yarn bodies, leather faces, and sunflower-seed beaks, but there the similarities end. Some have buttons for eyes, while others have glass. Some hold their wings tucked in to their sides, while others spread their speckled feathers in flight. They all have a splendid wide-eyed innocence, but beyond that, each little bird has a look and a personality all its own.

To make the owls, Tasha wraps yarn repeatedly around a piece of cardboard and then snips it into shape. She got the idea from the Victorian yarn balls she made for her children to toss back and forth when they were growing up. "It takes so little to keep a child amused," she often says. But the owls have come a long way from their roots. Of course, Tasha plays down the craftsmanship involved. "I just sculpt the yarn," she insists. "There's nothing to it, really. But don't get carried away with the scissors. Once you've made a cut, there's little redress." Each owl has a soft white breast that accents the tufts of ombre yarn that make up his body. Then Tasha glues two painted leather circles to his face and tucks down all around, because these are young screech owls that haven't yet lost their fledgling fluff. Guinea hen feathers stand upright for the "ears" and are also affixed as wings. Then she completes the creation with a pair of three-toed wire claws wrapped in white fabric. With the aid of a few strategically attached wires, the owls can perch wherever Tasha pleases. One or two always reside on her easel, overlooking whatever artwork happens to be in progress.

The easel is positioned at one end of a long wooden table that is laid with a feast during holidays. When not needed for dining, it serves as a workbench, pushed against the wall close to the windows. Tasha keeps innumerable bottles of paint and brushes of every dimension close by, and many bottles of ink and other artist's supplies are also within reach. Not far away sit a jar of feathers, several skeins of yarn, snippets of fabric, and all sorts of odd "finds" that Tasha has col-

Although Tasha has concocted dozens of little screech owls, no two are alike. They all have sunflower seed beaks, but each has a unique expression.

lected. The remainder of the table is taken up by toys in the making or their prototypes.

ALTHOUGH TASHA IS PARTIAL TO screech owls at present, she has made a stuffed, carved, or otherwise hand-constructed likeness of just about every animal that has ever ventured onto her property, as well as creatures that have never visited but that she fancies. There's Horatio Rabbit, impeccably dressed in a very fetching coat with a red vest, and Letitia O'Hare, with a gingham pinafore and harvest basket. Both are made of yarn with horsehair whiskers. Not far away sits Tokki O'Hare, also of yarn, with a perennially astonished expression on his face ("A bunny might look a little surprised nowadays, don't you think?"). Bethany's childhood velveteen magpie sits on the table waiting for repairs to its sagging tail, and a similarly designed brand-new felt crow dressed in vest and scarf perches nearby. Tasha made a long slinky cat to drape over her grandchildren's shoulders and carved a fine Nubian goat whose body she covered with an old flannel sheet painted the proper shades of fawn. Not only does the goat possess the characteristic Roman nose, floppy ears, and generous gut of Tasha's own dairy animals, but she also boasts a soft, pliable udder stuffed with cotton. In addition, the table holds several corgyn, a hedgehog, and quite a few mice and other rodents. But there is a con-

spicuous absence of chipmunks. Tasha has no wish to glorify the rascals who steal her flower bulbs and otherwise damage the garden.

Tasha never works on her watercolors after dark. "I need daylight to achieve the proper colors," she explains. Instead, when the sun goes down, she sits by the open hearth and works on a toy. The nearby loom displays a blue and white blanket in progress, the spinning wheel waits to fill a spare moment, and a newly made dress or two is spread proudly where it might be admired. There is always plenty to see and much to learn. And Tasha is the perfect teacher, patiently revealing the secrets of each task, surrounding her skills in a web of fantastic tales that add to their allure. Everything can be lighthearted. Everything can be done with integrity. The fire sends out shadows that dance on Tasha's face and accentuate her cheekbones as she concentrates on whatever she is meticulously working at — with hands that are never idle.